I0004041

Applied Data Science with Python and Jupyter

Use powerful industry-standard tools to unlock new, actionable insights from your data

Alex Galea

Applied Data Science with Python and Jupyter

Copyright © 2018 Packt Publishing

All rights reserved. No part of this book may be reproduced, stored in a retrieval system, or transmitted in any form or by any means, without the prior written permission of the publisher, except in the case of brief quotations embedded in critical articles or reviews.

Every effort has been made in the preparation of this book to ensure the accuracy of the information presented. However, the information contained in this book is sold without warranty, either express or implied. Neither the author, nor Packt Publishing, and its dealers and distributors will be held liable for any damages caused or alleged to be caused directly or indirectly by this book.

Packt Publishing has endeavored to provide trademark information about all of the companies and products mentioned in this book by the appropriate use of capitals. However, Packt Publishing cannot guarantee the accuracy of this information.

Author: Alex Galea

Reviewer: Elie Kawerk

Managing Editor: Mahesh Dhyani

Acquisitions Editor: Aditya Date

Production Editor: Samita Warang

Editorial Board: David Barnes, Ewan Buckingham, Simon Cox, Manasa Kumar, Alex Mazonowicz, Douglas Paterson, Dominic Pereira, Shiny Poojary, Saman Siddiqui, Erol Staveley, Ankita Thakur, and Mohita Vyas

First Published: October 2018

Production Reference: 2051218

ISBN: 978-1-78995-817-1

Table of Contents

Preface

About

This section briefly introduces the author, the coverage of this book, the technical skills you'll need to get started, and the hardware and software requirements required to complete all of the included activities and exercises.

About the Book

Applied Data Science with Python and Jupyter teaches you the skills you need for entry-level data science. You'll learn about some of the most commonly used libraries that are part of the Anaconda distribution, and then explore machine learning models with real datasets to give you the skills and exposure you need for the real world. You'll finish up by learning how easy it can be to scrape and gather your own data from the open web so that you can apply your new skills in an actionable context.

About the Author

Alex Galea has been doing data analysis professionally since graduating with a master's in physics from the University of Guelph in Canada. He developed a keen interest in Python while researching quantum gases as part of his graduate studies. More recently, Alex has been doing web data analytics, where Python continues to play a large part in his work. He frequently blogs about work and personal projects, which are generally data-centric and usually involve Python and Jupyter Notebooks.

Objectives

- Get up and running with the Jupyter ecosystem
- Identify potential areas of investigation and perform exploratory data analysis
- Plan a machine learning classification strategy and train classification models
- Use validation curves and dimensionality reduction to tune and enhance your models
- Scrape tabular data from web pages and transform it into Pandas DataFrames
- Create interactive, web-friendly visualizations to clearly communicate your findings

Audience

Applied Data Science with Python and Jupyter is ideal for professionals with a variety of job descriptions across a large range of industries, given the rising popularity and accessibility of data science. You'll need some prior experience with Python, with any prior work with libraries such as Pandas, Matplotlib, and Pandas providing you a useful head start.

Approach

Applied Data Science with Python and Jupyter covers every aspect of the standard data workflow process with a perfect blend of theory, practical hands-on coding, and relatable illustrations. Each module is designed to build on the learnings of the previous chapter. The book contains multiple activities that use real-life business scenarios for you to practice and apply your new skills in a highly relevant context.

Minimum Hardware Requirements

The minimum hardware requirements are as follows:

- Processor: Intel i5 (or equivalent)
- Memory: 8 GB RAM
- Hard disk: 10 GB
- An internet connection

Software Requirements

You'll also need the following software installed in advance:

- Python 3.5+
- Anaconda 4.3+
- Python libraries included with Anaconda installation:
- matplotlib 2.1.0+
- ipython 6.1.0+
- requests 2.18.4+
- beautifulsoup4 4.6.0+
- numpy 1.13.1+
- pandas 0.20.3+
- scikit-learn 0.19.0+
- seaborn 0.8.0+
- bokeh 0.12.10+
- Python libraries that require manual installation:
- mlxtend
- version_information

- ipython-sql
- pdir2
- graphviz

Installation and Setup

Before you start with this book, we'll install Anaconda environment which consists of Python and Jupyter Notebook.

Installing Anaconda

1. Visit https://www.anaconda.com/download/ in your browser.
2. Click on Windows, Mac, or Linux, depending on the OS you are working on.
3. Next, click on the Download option. Make sure you download the latest version.
4. Open the installer after download.
5. Follow the steps in the installer and that's it! Your Anaconda distribution is ready.

Updating Jupyter and Installing Dependencies

1. Search for Anaconda Prompt and open it.
2. Type the following commands to update conda and Jupyter:

```
#Update conda
conda update conda

#Update Jupyter
conda update Jupyter

#install packages
conda install numpy
conda install pandas
conda install statsmodels
conda install matplotlib
conda install seaborn
```

3. To open Jupyter Notebook from Anaconda Prompt, use the following command:

```
jupyter notebook
pip install -U scikit-learn
```

Additional Resources

The code bundle for this book is also hosted on GitHub at https://github.com/TrainingByPackt/Applied-Data-Science-with-Python-and-Jupyter.

We also have other code bundles from our rich catalog of books and videos available at https://github.com/PacktPublishing/. Check them out!

Conventions

Code words in text, database table names, folder names, filenames, file extensions, path names, dummy URLs, user input, and Twitter handles are shown as follows:

"The final figure is then saved as a high resolution PNG to the **figures** folder."

A block of code is set as follows:

```
y = df['MEDV'].copy()
del df['MEDV']
df = pd.concat((y, df), axis=1)
```

Any command-line input or output is written as follows:

```
jupyter notebook
```

New terms and important words are shown in bold. Words that you see on the

screen, for example, in menus or dialog boxes, appear in the text like this: "Click on **New** in the upper-right corner and select a kernel from the drop-down menu."

Jupyter Fundamentals

Learning Objectives

By the end of this chapter, you will be able to:

- Describe Jupyter Notebooks and how they are used for data analysis
- Describe the features of Jupyter Notebooks
- Use Python data science libraries
- Perform simple exploratory data analysis

In this chapter, you will learn and implement the fundamental features of the Jupyter notebook by completing several hands-on erxercises.

Introduction

Jupyter Notebooks are one of the most important tools for data scientists using Python. This is because they're an ideal environment for developing reproducible data analysis pipelines. Data can be loaded, transformed, and modeled all inside a single Notebook, where it's quick and easy to test out code and explore ideas along the way. Furthermore, all of this can be documented "inline" using formatted text, so you can make notes for yourself or even produce a structured report.

Other comparable platforms - for example, RStudio or Spyder - present the user with multiple windows, which promote arduous tasks such as copy and pasting code around and rerunning code that has already been executed. These tools also tend to involve **Read Eval Prompt Loops** (**REPLs**) where code is run in a terminal session that has saved memory. This type of development environment is bad for reproducibility and not ideal for development either. Jupyter Notebooks solve all these issues by giving the user a single window where code snippets are executed and outputs are displayed inline. This lets users develop code efficiently and allows them to look back at previous work for reference, or even to make alterations.

We'll start the chapter by explaining exactly what Jupyter Notebooks are and continue to discuss why they are so popular among data scientists. Then, we'll open a Notebook together and go through some exercises to learn how the platform is used. Finally, we'll dive into our first analysis and perform an exploratory analysis in

Basic Functionality and Features

In this section, we first demonstrate the usefulness of Jupyter Notebooks with examples and through discussion. Then, in order to cover the fundamentals of Jupyter Notebooks for beginners, we'll see the basic usage of them in terms of launching and interacting with the platform. For those who have used Jupyter Notebooks before, this will be mostly a review; however, you will certainly see new things in this topic as well.

What is a Jupyter Notebook and Why is it Useful?

Jupyter Notebooks are locally run web applications which contain live code, equations, figures, interactive apps, and **Markdown** text. The standard language is Python, and that's what we'll be using for this book; however, note that a variety of alternatives are supported. This includes the other dominant data science language, R:

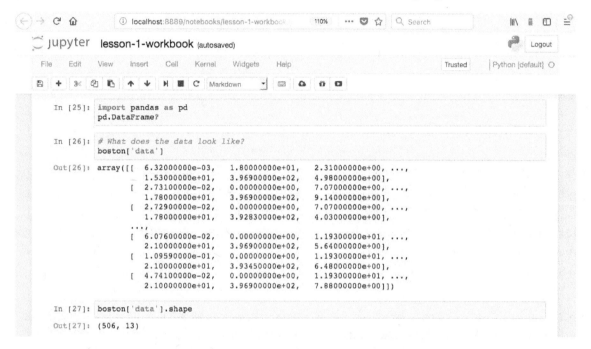

Figure 1.1: Jupyter Notebook sample workbook

Those familiar with R will know about R Markdown. **Markdown** documents allow for Markdown-formatted text to be combined with executable code. **Markdown** is a simple language used for styling text on the web. For example, most GitHub repositories have a `README.md` **Markdown** file. This format is useful for basic text formatting. It's comparable to HTML but allows for much less customization.

Commonly used symbols in **Markdown** include hashes (#) to make text into a heading, square and round brackets to insert hyperlinks, and stars to create italicized or bold text:

```
# Markdown!

This is a basic [Markdown]
(https://en.wikipedia.org/wiki/Markdown) document.

### Sub heading

It's *simple*, but **powerful**.
```

Markdown!

This is a basic Markdown document.

Sub heading

It's *simple*, but **powerful**.

Figure 1.2: Sample Markdown document

Having seen the basics of Markdown, let's come back to R Markdown, where **Markdown** text can be written alongside executable code. Jupyter Notebooks offer the equivalent functionality for Python, although, as we'll see, they function quite differently than R **Markdown** documents. For example, R **Markdown** assumes you are writing **Markdown** unless otherwise specified, whereas Jupyter Notebooks assume you are inputting code. This makes it more appealing to use Jupyter Notebooks for rapid development and testing.

From a data science perspective, there are two primary types for a Jupyter Notebook depending on how they are used: lab-style and deliverable.

Lab-style Notebooks are meant to serve as the programming analog of research journals. These should contain all the work you've done to load, process, analyze, and model the data. The idea here is to document everything you've done for future reference, so it's usually not advisable to delete or alter previous lab-style Notebooks. It's also a good idea to accumulate multiple date-stamped versions of the Notebook as you progress through the analysis, in case you want to look back at previous states.

Deliverable Notebooks are intended to be presentable and should contain only select parts of the lab-style Notebooks. For example, this could be an interesting discovery to share with your colleagues, an in-depth report of your analysis for a manager, or a summary of the key findings for stakeholders.

In either case, an important concept is reproducibility. If you've been diligent in documenting your software versions, anyone receiving the reports will be able to rerun the Notebook and compute the same results as you did. In the scientific community, where reproducibility is becoming increasingly difficult, this is a breath of fresh air.

Navigating the Platform

Now, we are going to open up a Jupyter Notebook and start to learn the interface. Here, we will assume you have no prior knowledge of the platform and go over the basic usage.

Exercise 1: Introducing Jupyter Notebooks

1. Navigate to the companion material directory in the terminal

> **Note**
>
> Unix machines such as Mac or Linux, command-line navigation can be done using **ls** to display directory contents and **cd** to change directories. On Windows machines, use **dir** to display directory contents and use cd to change directories instead. If, for example, you want to change the drive from C: to D:, you should execute d: to change drives.

2. Start a new local Notebook server here by typing the following into the terminal:

    ```
    jupyter notebook
    ```

    A new window or tab of your default browser will open the Notebook Dashboard to the working directory. Here, you will see a list of folders and files contained therein.

3. Click on a folder to navigate to that particular path and open a file by clicking on it. Although its main use is editing IPYNB Notebook files, Jupyter functions as a standard text editor as well.

4. Reopen the terminal window used to launch the app. We can see the **NotebookApp** being run on a local server. In particular, you should see a line like this:

    ```
    [I 20:03:01.045 NotebookApp] The Jupyter Notebook is running at: http://
    localhost:8888/?token=e915bb06866f19ce462d959a9193a94c7c088e81765f9d8a
    ```

    Going to that HTTP address will load the app in your browser window, as was done automatically when starting the app. Closing the window does not stop the app; this should be done from the terminal by typing *Ctrl* + *C*.

5. Close the app by typing *Ctrl* + *C* in the terminal. You may also have to confirm by entering **y**. Close the web browser window as well.

6. Load the list of available options by running the following code:

    ```
    jupyter notebook --help
    ```

7. Open the **NotebookApp** at local port **9000** by running the following:

    ```
    jupyter notebook --port 9000
    ```

8. Click **New** in the upper-right corner of the Jupyter Dashboard and select a kernel from the drop-down menu (that is, select something in the **Notebooks** section):

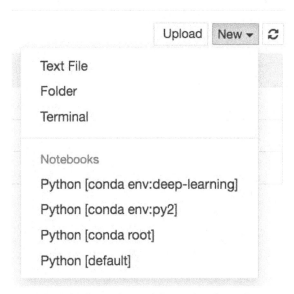

Figure 1.3: Selecting a kernel from the drop down menu

This is the primary method of creating a new Jupyter Notebook.

Kernels provide programming language support for the Notebook. If you have installed Python with Anaconda, that version should be the default kernel. Conda virtual environments will also be available here.

> **Note**
>
> Virtual environments are a great tool for managing multiple projects on the same machine. Each virtual environment may contain a different version of Python and external libraries. Python has built-in virtual environments; however, the Conda virtual environment integrates better with Jupyter Notebooks and boasts other nice features. The documentation is available at: https://conda.io/docs/user-guide/tasks/manage-environments.html.

9. With the newly created blank Notebook, click the top cell and type `print('hello world')`, or any other code snippet that writes to the screen.

10. Click the cell and press *Shift + Enter* or select **Run Cell** in the **Cell** menu.

    Any `stdout` or `stderr` output from the code will be displayed beneath as the cell runs. Furthermore, the string representation of the object written in the final line will be displayed as well. This is very handy, especially for displaying tables, but sometimes we don't want the final object to be displayed. In such cases, a semicolon (;) can be added to the end of the line to suppress the display. New cells expect and run code input by default; however, they can be changed to render **Markdown** instead.

11. Click an empty cell and change it to accept the Markdown-formatted text. This can be done from the drop-down menu icon in the toolbar or by selecting **Markdown** from the **Cell** menu. Write some text in here (any text will do), making sure to utilize Markdown formatting symbols such as #.

12. Scroll to the **Play** icon in the tool bar:

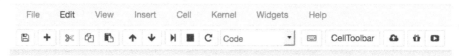

Figure 1.4: Jupyter Notebook tool bar

This can be used to run cells. As we'll see later, however, it's handier to use the keyboard shortcut *Shift + Enter* to run cells.

Right next to this is a **Stop** icon, which can be used to stop cells from running. This is useful, for example, if a cell is taking too long to run:

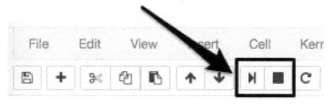

Figure 1.5: Stop icon in Jupyter Notebooks

New cells can be manually added from the **Insert** menu:

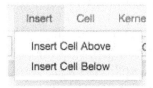

Figure 1.6: Adding new cells from the Insert menu in Jupyter Notebooks

Cells can be copied, pasted, and deleted using icons or by selecting options from the **Edit** menu:

Figure 1.7: Edit Menu in the Jupyter Notebooks

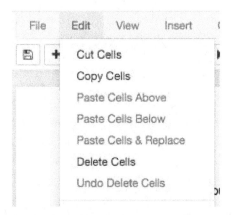

Figure 1.8: Cutting and copying cells in Jupyter Notebooks

Cells can also be moved up and down this way:

Figure 1.9: Moving cells up and down in Jupyter Notebooks

There are useful options under the **Cell** menu to run a group of cells or the entire Notebook:

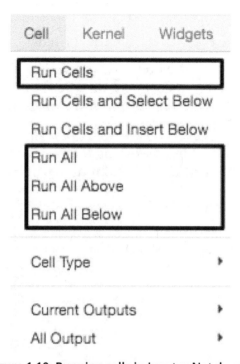

Figure 1.10: Running cells in Jupyter Notebooks

Experiment with the toolbar options to move cells up and down, insert new cells, and delete cells. An important thing to understand about these Notebooks is the shared memory between cells. It's quite simple: every cell existing on the sheet has access to the global set of variables. So, for example, a function defined in one cell could be called from any other, and the same applies to variables. As one would expect, anything within the scope of a function will not be a global variable and can only be accessed from within that specific function.

13. Open the **Kernel** menu to see the selections. The **Kernel** menu is useful for stopping script executions and restarting the Notebook if the kernel dies. Kernels can also be swapped here at any time, but it is unadvisable to use multiple kernels for a single Notebook due to reproducibility concerns.

14. Open the **File** menu to see the selections. The **File** menu contains options for downloading the Notebook in various formats. In particular, it's recommended to save an HTML version of your Notebook, where the content is rendered statically and can be opened and viewed "as you would expect" in web browsers.

The Notebook name will be displayed in the upper-left corner. New Notebooks will automatically be named **Untitled**.

15. Change the name of your IPYNB Notebook file by clicking on the current name in the upper-left corner and typing the new name. Then, save the file.

16. Close the current tab in your web browser (exiting the Notebook) and go to the **Jupyter Dashboard** tab, which should still be open. (If it's not open, then reload it by copy and pasting the HTTP link from the terminal.)

    Since we didn't shut down the Notebook, and we just saved and exited, it will have a green book symbol next to its name in the **Files** section of the Jupyter Dashboard and will be listed as **Running** on the right side next to the last modified date. Notebooks can be shut down from here.

17. Quit the Notebook you have been working on by selecting it (checkbox to the left of the name), and then click the orange **Shutdown** button:

> **Note**
>
> Read through the basic keyboard shortcuts and test them.

Figure 1.11: Shutting down the Jupyter notebook

> **Note**
>
> If you plan to spend a lot of time working with Jupyter Notebooks, it's worthwhile to learn the keyboard shortcuts. This will speed up your workflow considerably. Particularly useful commands to learn are the shortcuts for manually adding new cells and converting cells from code to Markdown formatting. Click on **Keyboard Shortcuts** from the **Help** menu to see how.

Jupyter Features

Jupyter has many appealing features that make for efficient Python programming. These include an assortment of things, from methods for viewing docstrings to executing Bash commands. We will explore some of these features in this section.

> **Note**
>
> The official IPython documentation can be found here: http://ipython.readthedocs. io/en/stable/. It has details on the features we will discuss here and others.

Exercise 2: Implementing Jupyter's Most Useful Features

1. Navigate to the **lesson-1** directory from the Jupyter Dashboard and open **lesson-1-workbook.ipynb** by selecting it.

    The standard file extension for Jupyter Notebooks is **.ipynb**, which was introduced back when they were called IPython Notebooks.

2. Scroll down to **Subtopic C: Jupyter Features** in the Jupyter Notebook.

    We start by reviewing the basic keyboard shortcuts. These are especially helpful to avoid having to use the mouse so often, which will greatly speed up the workflow.

    You can get help by adding a question mark to the end of any object and running the cell. Jupyter finds the docstring for that object and returns it in a pop-out window at the bottom of the app.

3. Run the **Getting Help** cell and check how Jupyter displays the docstrings at the bottom of the Notebook. Add a cell in this section and get help on the object of your choice:

Getting Help

- add question mark to end of object

```
In [3]:  # Get the numpy arange docstring
         import numpy as np
         np.arange?
```

```
Docstring:
arange([start,] stop[, step,], dtype=None)

Return evenly spaced values within a given interval.

Values are generated within the half-open interval ``[start, stop)``
(in other words, the interval including `start` but excluding `stop`).
For integer arguments the function is equivalent to the Python built-in
`range <http://docs.python.org/lib/built-in-funcs.html>`_ function,
but returns an ndarray rather than a list.
```

Figure 1.12: Getting help in Jupyter Notebooks

4. Click an empty code cell in the **Tab Completion** section. Type import (including the space after) and then press the **Tab** key:

Tab Completion

Example of Jupyter tab completion include:

- listing available modules on import
  ```
  import <tab>
  from numpy import <tab>
  ```
- listing available modules after import
  ```
  np.<tab>
  ```

Figure 1.13: Tab completion in Jupyter Notebooks

The above action listed all the available modules for import.

Tab completion can be used for the following: **list available modules when importing external libraries**; **list available modules of imported external libraries**; **function and variable completion**. This can be especially useful when you need to know the available input arguments for a module, when exploring a new library, to discover new modules, or simply to speed up workflow. They will save time writing out variable names or functions and reduce bugs from typos. The tab completion works so well that you may have difficulty coding Python in other editors after today!

5. Scroll to the Jupyter Magic Functions section and run the cells containing `%lsmagic` and `%matplotlib` inline:

Jupyter Magic Functions

List of the available magic commands:

```
%lsmagic
```

```
Available line magics:
%alias  %alias_magic  %autocall  %automagic  %auto
ist  %dirs  %doctest_mode  %ed  %edit  %env  %gui
dpy  %logoff  %logon  %logstart  %logstate  %logst
ook  %page  %pastebin  %pdb  %pdef  %pdoc  %pfile
ushd  %pwd  %pycat  %pylab  %qtconsole  %quickref
%run  %save  %sc  %set_env  %store  %sx  %system
```

Figure 1.14: Jupyter Magic functions

The percent signs, % and %%, are one of the basic features of Jupyter Notebook and are called magic commands. Magics starting with `%%` will apply to the entire cell, and magics starting with `%` will only apply to that line.

`%lsmagic` lists the available options. We will discuss and show examples of some of the most useful ones. The most common magic command you will probably see is `%matplotlib` inline, which allows matplotlib figures to be displayed in the Notebook without having to explicitly use `plt.show()`.

The timing functions are very handy and come in two varieties: a standard timer (**%time** or **%%time**) and a timer that measures the average runtime of many iterations (**%timeit** and **%%timeit**).

> **Note**
>
> Notice how list comprehensions are quicker than loops in Python. This can be seen by comparing the wall time for the first and second cell, where the same calculation is done significantly faster with the list comprehension.

6. Run the cells in the **Timers** section.

   Note the difference between using one and two percent signs. Even by using a Python kernel (as you are currently doing), other languages can be invoked using magic commands. The built-in options include JavaScript, R, Pearl, Ruby, and Bash. Bash is particularly useful, as you can use Unix commands to find out where you are currently (**pwd**), what's in the directory (**ls**), make new folders (**mkdir**), and write file contents (**cat/head/tail**).

7. Run the first cell in the **Using bash** in the notebook section.

   This cell writes some text to a file in the working directory, prints the directory contents, prints an empty line, and then writes back the contents of the newly created file before removing it:

Using bash in the notebook

```
In [9]: %%bash

echo "using bash from inside Jupyter!" > test-file.txt
ls
echo ""
cat test-file.txt
rm test-file.txt
```

```
Lesson 1
Lesson 1.docx
Lesson 1.pptx
lesson-1-workbook.html
lesson-1-workbook.ipynb
test-file.txt
~$sson 1.docx

using bash from inside Jupyter!
```

Figure 1.15: Using Bash in Jupyter Notebooks

8. Run the cells containing only **ls** and **pwd**.

Note how we did not have to explicitly use the Bash magic command for these to work. There are plenty of external magic commands that can be installed. A popular one is **ipython-sql**, which allows for SQL code to be executed in cells.

9. Open a new terminal window and execute the following code to install ipython-sql:

```
pip install ipython-sql
```

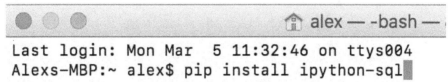

```
Last login: Mon Mar  5 11:32:46 on ttys004
Alexs-MBP:~ alex$ pip install ipython-sql
```

Figure 1.16: Installing ipython-sql using pip

10. Run the **%load_ext sql** cell to load the external command into the Notebook:

```
: # Source: https://github.com/catherinedevlin/ipython-sql
  # do pip install ipython-sql in the terminal
  %load_ext sql
```

Figure 1.17: Loading sql in Jupyter Notebooks

This allows for connections to remote databases so that queries can be executed (and thereby documented) right inside the Notebook.

11. Run the cell containing the SQL sample query:

```
%%sql sqlite://

SELECT *
FROM (
    SELECT 'Hello' as msg_1
) A JOIN (
    SELECT 'World!' as msg_2
) B;
```

Done.

msg_1	msg_2
Hello	World!

Figure 1.18: Running a sample SQL query

Here, we first connect to the local sqlite source; however, this line could instead point to a specific database on a local or remote server. Then, we execute a simple **SELECT** to show how the cell has been converted to run SQL code instead of Python.

12. Install the version documentation tool now from the terminal using **pip**. Open up a new window and run the following code:

```
pip install version_information
```

Once installed, it can then be imported into any Notebook using **%load_ext version_information**. Finally, once loaded, it can be used to display the versions of each piece of software in the Notebook.

The **%version_information commands helps with documentation**, but it does not come as standard with Jupyter. Like the SQL example we just saw, it can be installed from the command line with **pip**.

13. Run the cell that loads and calls the **version_information** command:

```
%load_ext version_information
%version_information requests, numpy, pandas, matplotlib, seaborn, sklearn
```

Software	Version
Python	3.5.4 64bit [GCC 4.2.1 Compatible Clang 4.0.1 (tags/RELEASE_401/final)]
IPython	6.1.0
OS	Darwin 16.5.0 x86_64 i386 64bit
requests	2.18.4
numpy	1.13.1
pandas	0.20.3
matplotlib	2.0.2
seaborn	0.8.0
sklearn	0.19.0
Wed Oct 11 19:46:08 2017 PDT	

Figure 1.19: Version Information in Jupyter

Converting a Jupyter Notebook to a Python Script

You can convert a Jupyter Notebook to a Python script. This is equivalent to copying and pasting the contents of each code cell into a single **.py** file. The Markdown sections are also included as comments.

The conversion can be done from the **NotebookApp** or in the command line as follows:

```
jupyter nbconvert --to=python lesson-1-notebook.ipynb
```

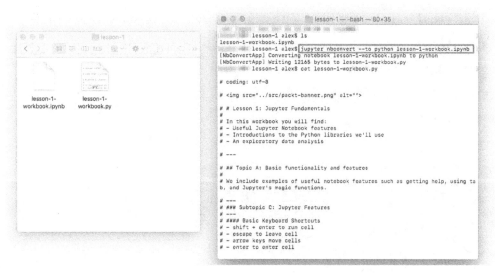

Figure 1.20: Converting a Jupyter Notebook into a Python Script

This is useful, for example, when you want to determine the library requirements for a Notebook using a tool such as **pipreqs**. This tool determines the libraries used in a project and exports them into a **requirements.txt** file (and it can be installed by running pip install **pipreqs**).

The command is called from outside the folder containing your **.py** files. For example, if the **.py** files are inside a folder called **lesson-1**, you could do the following:

```
pipreqs lesson-1/
```

Figure 1.21: Determining library requirements using pipreqs

The resulting **requirements.txt** file for **lesson-1-workbook.ipynb** looks like this:

```
cat lesson-1/requirements.txt

matplotlib==2.0.2 numpy==1.13.1

pandas==0.20.3

requests==2.18.4

seaborn==0.8

beautifulsoup4==4.6.0

scikit_learn==0.19.0
```

Python Libraries

Having now seen all the basics of Jupyter Notebooks, and even some more advanced features, we'll shift our attention to the Python libraries we'll be using in this book. Libraries, in general, extend the default set of Python functions. Examples of commonly used standard libraries are `datetime`, `time`, and `os`. These are called standard libraries because they come standard with every installation of Python.

For data science with Python, the most important libraries are external, which means they do not come standard with Python.

The external data science libraries we'll be using in this book are NumPy, Pandas, Seaborn, matplotlib, scikit-learn, Requests, and Bokeh.

> **Note**
>
> A word of caution: It's a good idea to import libraries using industry standards, for example, import numpy as np; this way, your code is more readable. Try to avoid doing things such as from numpy import *, as you may unwittingly overwrite functions. Furthermore, it's often nice to have modules linked to the library via a dot (.) for code readability.

Let's briefly introduce each.

- **NumPy** offers multi-dimensional data structures (arrays) on which operations can be performed far quicker than standard Python data structures (for example, lists). This is done in part by performing operations in the background using C. NumPy also offers various mathematical and data manipulation functions.

- **Pandas** is Python's answer to the R DataFrame. It stores data in 2D tabular structures where columns represent different variables and rows correspond to samples. Pandas provides many handy tools for data wrangling such as filling in **NaN** entries and computing statistical descriptions of the data. Working with Pandas DataFrames will be a big focus of this book.

- **Matplotlib** is a plotting tool inspired by the MATLAB platform. Those familiar with R can think of it as Python's version of ggplot. It's the most popular Python library for plotting figures and allows for a high level of customization.

- **Seaborn** works as an extension to matplotlib, where various plotting tools useful for data science are included. Generally speaking, this allows for analysis to be done much faster than if you were to create the same things *manually* with libraries such as matplotlib and scikit-learn.

- **scikit-learn** is the most commonly used machine learning library. It offers top-of-the-line algorithms and a very elegant API where models are instantiated and then *fit* with data. It also provides data processing modules and other tools useful for predictive analytics.

- **Requests** is the go-to library for making HTTP requests. It makes it straightforward to get HTML from web pages and interface with APIs. For parsing the HTML, many choose BeautifulSoup4, which we will also cover in this book.

- **Bokeh** is an interactive visualization library. It functions similar to matplotlib, but allows us to add hover, zoom, click, and use other interactive tools to our plots. It also allows us to render and play with the plots inside our Jupyter Notebook.

Having introduced these libraries, let's go back to our Notebook and load them, by running the `import` statements. This will lead us into our first analysis, where we finally start working with a dataset.

Exercise 3: Importing the External Libraries and Setting Up the Plotting Environment

1. Open up the `lesson 1` Jupyter Notebook and scroll to the `Subtopic D: Python Libraries` section.

   Just like for regular Python scripts, libraries can be imported into the Notebook at any time. It's best practice to put the majority of the packages you use at the top of the file. Sometimes it makes sense to load things midway through the Notebook and that is completely fine.

2. Run the cells to import the external libraries and set the plotting options:

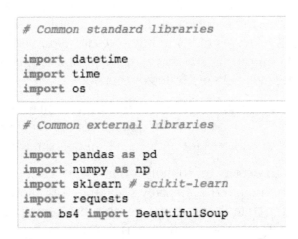

```
# Common standard libraries

import datetime
import time
import os
```

```
# Common external libraries

import pandas as pd
import numpy as np
import sklearn # scikit-learn
import requests
from bs4 import BeautifulSoup
```

Figure 1.22: Importing Python libraries

For a nice Notebook setup, it's often useful to set various options along with the imports at the top. For example, the following can be run to change the figure appearance to something more aesthetically pleasing than the matplotlib and Seaborn defaults:

```
import matplotlib.pyplot as plt

%matplotlib inline import

seaborn as sns


# See here for more options: https://matplotlib.org/users/ customizing.html

%config InlineBackend.figure_format='retina'

sns.set() # Revert to matplotlib defaults

plt.rcParams['figure.figsize'] = (9, 6)

plt.rcParams['axes.labelpad'] = 10 sns.set_style("darkgrid")
```

So far in this book, we've gone over the basics of using Jupyter Notebooks for data science. We started by exploring the platform and finding our way around the interface. Then, we discussed the most useful features, which include tab completion and magic functions. Finally, we introduced the Python libraries we'll be using in this book.

The next section will be very interactive as we perform our first analysis together using the Jupyter Notebook.

Our First Analysis - The Boston Housing Dataset

So far, this chapter has focused on the features and basic usage of Jupyter. Now, we'll put this into practice and do some data exploration and analysis.

The dataset we'll look at in this section is the so-called Boston housing dataset. It contains US census data concerning houses in various areas around the city of Boston. Each sample corresponds to a unique area and has about a dozen measures. We should think of samples as rows and measures as columns. The data was first published in 1978 and is quite small, containing only about 500 samples.

Now that we know something about the context of the dataset, let's decide on a rough plan for the exploration and analysis. If applicable, this plan would accommodate the relevant question(s) under study. In this case, the goal is not to answer a question but to instead show Jupyter in action and illustrate some basic data analysis methods.

Our general approach to this analysis will be to do the following:

- Load the data into Jupyter using a Pandas DataFrame
- Quantitatively understand the features
- Look for patterns and generate questions
- Answer the questions to the problems

Loading the Data into Jupyter Using a Pandas DataFrame

Oftentimes, data is stored in tables, which means it can be saved as a **comma-separated variable** (**CSV**) file. This format, and many others, can be read into Python as a DataFrame object, using the Pandas library. Other common formats include **tab-separated variable** (**TSV**), SQL tables, and JSON data structures. Indeed, Pandas has support for all of these. In this example, however, we are not going to load the data this way because the dataset is available directly through scikit-learn.

> **Note**
>
> An important part after loading data for analysis is ensuring that it's clean. For example, we would generally need to deal with missing data and ensure that all columns have the correct datatypes. The dataset we use in this section has already been cleaned, so we will not need to worry about this. However, we'll see messier data in the second chapter and explore techniques for dealing with it.

Exercise 4: Loading the Boston Housing Dataset

1. Scroll to **Subtopic A** of **Topic B: Our first Analysis: the Boston Housing Dataset** in chapter 1 of the Jupyter Notebook.

   The Boston housing dataset can be accessed from the `sklearn.datasets` module using the `load_boston` method.

2. Run the first two cells in this section to load the Boston dataset and see the **datastructures** type:

```
from sklearn import datasets
boston = datasets.load_boston()
```

```
type(boston)
```

```
sklearn.utils.Bunch
```

Figure 1.23: Loading the Boston dataset

The output of the second cell tells us that it's a scikit-learn **Bunch** object. Let's get some more information about that to understand what we are dealing with.

3. Run the next cell to import the base object from scikit-learn **utils** and print the docstring in our Notebook:

```
In [4]:  from sklearn.utils import Bunch
         Bunch?
```

```
Init signature: Bunch(**kwargs)
Docstring:
Container object for datasets

Dictionary-like object that exposes its keys as attributes.

>>> b = Bunch(a=1, b=2)
>>> b['b']
2
```

Figure 1.24: Importing base objects and printing the docstring

4. Print the field names (that is, the keys to the dictionary) by running the next cell. We find these fields to be self-explanatory: `['DESCR', 'target', 'data', 'feature_names']`.

5. Run the next cell to print the dataset description contained in **boston['DESCR']**.

   Note that in this call, we explicitly want to print the field value so that the Notebook renders the content in a more readable format than the string representation (that is, if we just type **boston['DESCR']** without wrapping it in a **print** statement). We then see the dataset information as we've previously summarized:

   ```
   Boston House Prices dataset
   ===========================

   Notes
   ------
   Data Set Characteristics:

    :Number of Instances: 506
    :Number of Attributes: 13 numeric/categorical predictive
    :Median Value (attribute 14) is usually the target
    :Attribute Information (in order):
    - CRIM      per capita crime rate by town
    ...

    ...
    - MEDV      Median value of owner-occupied homes in $1000's
    :Missing Attribute Values: None
   ```

   > **Note**
   >
   > Briefly read through the feature descriptions and/or describe them yourself. For the purposes of this tutorial, the most important fields to understand are **RM**, **AGE**, **LSTAT**, and **MEDV**. Note down the important variables that we will use in the dataset, such as **RM**, **AGE**, **LSTAT**, and **MEDV**.

   Of particular importance here are the feature descriptions (under **Attribute Information**). We will use this as reference during our analysis.

   > **Note**
   >
   > For the complete code, refer to the following: https://bit.ly/2EL11cW

Now, we are going to create a Pandas DataFrame that contains the data. This is beneficial for a few reasons: all of our data will be contained in one object, there are useful and computationally efficient DataFrame methods we can use, and other libraries such as Seaborn have tools that integrate nicely with DataFrames.

In this case, we will create our DataFrame with the standard constructor method.

6. Run the cell where Pandas is imported and the docstring is retrieved for **pd.DataFrame:**

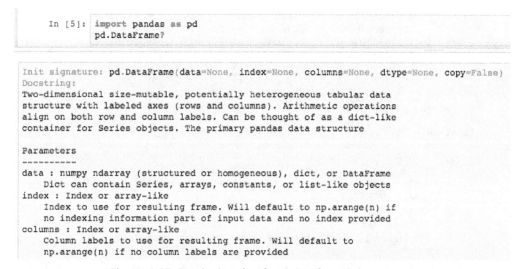

```
In [5]: import pandas as pd
        pd.DataFrame?
```

```
Init signature: pd.DataFrame(data=None, index=None, columns=None, dtype=None, copy=False)
Docstring:
Two-dimensional size-mutable, potentially heterogeneous tabular data
structure with labeled axes (rows and columns). Arithmetic operations
align on both row and column labels. Can be thought of as a dict-like
container for Series objects. The primary pandas data structure

Parameters
----------
data : numpy ndarray (structured or homogeneous), dict, or DataFrame
    Dict can contain Series, arrays, constants, or list-like objects
index : Index or array-like
    Index to use for resulting frame. Will default to np.arange(n) if
    no indexing information part of input data and no index provided
columns : Index or array-like
    Column labels to use for resulting frame. Will default to
    np.arange(n) if no column labels are provided
```

Figure 1.25: Retrieving the docstring for pd.DataFrame

The docstring reveals the DataFrame input parameters. We want to feed in **boston['data']** for the data and use **boston['feature_names']** for the headers.

7. Run the next few cells to print the data, its shape, and the feature names:

```
# What does the data look like?
boston['data']

array([[  6.32000000e-03,   1.80000000e+01,   2.31000000e+00, ...,
          1.53000000e+01,   3.96900000e+02,   4.98000000e+00],
       [  2.73100000e-02,   0.00000000e+00,   7.07000000e+00, ...,
          1.78000000e+01,   3.96900000e+02,   9.14000000e+00],
       [  2.72900000e-02,   0.00000000e+00,   7.07000000e+00, ...,
          1.78000000e+01,   3.92830000e+02,   4.03000000e+00],
       ...,
       [  6.07600000e-02,   0.00000000e+00,   1.19300000e+01, ...,
          2.10000000e+01,   3.96900000e+02,   5.64000000e+00],
       [  1.09590000e-01,   0.00000000e+00,   1.19300000e+01, ...,
          2.10000000e+01,   3.93450000e+02,   6.48000000e+00],
       [  4.74100000e-02,   0.00000000e+00,   1.19300000e+01, ...,
          2.10000000e+01,   3.96900000e+02,   7.88000000e+00]])
```

```
boston['data'].shape
```

```
(506, 13)
```

```
boston['feature_names']
```

```
array(['CRIM', 'ZN', 'INDUS', 'CHAS', 'NOX', 'RM', 'AGE', 'DIS', 'RAD',
       'TAX', 'PTRATIO', 'B', 'LSTAT'],
      dtype='<U7')
```

Figure 1.26: Printing data, shape, and feature names

Looking at the output, we see that our data is in a 2D NumPy array. Running the command **boston['data']**.**shape** returns the length (number of samples) and the number of features as the first and second outputs, respectively.

8. Load the data into a Pandas DataFrame **df** by running the following:

```
df = pd.DataFrame(data=boston['data'],
columns=boston['feature_names'])
```

In machine learning, the variable that is being modeled is called the target variable; it's what you are trying to predict given the features. For this dataset, the suggested target is **MEDV**, the median house value in 1,000s of dollars.

9. Run the next cell to see the shape of the target:

```
# Still need to add the target variable
boston['target'].shape
```

```
(506,)
```

Figure 1.27: Code for viewing the shape of the target

We see that it has the same length as the features, which is what we expect. It can therefore be added as a new column to the DataFrame.

10. Add the target variable to df by running the cell with the following:

```
df['MEDV'] = boston['target']
```

11. Move the target variable to the front of **df** by running the cell with the following code:

```
y = df['MEDV'].copy()
del df['MEDV']
df = pd.concat((y, df), axis=1)
```

This is done to distinguish the target from our features by storing it to the front of our DataFrame.

Here, we introduce a dummy variable **y** to hold a copy of the target column before removing it from the DataFrame. We then use the Pandas concatenation function to combine it with the remaining DataFrame along the 1st axis (as opposed to the 0th axis, which combines rows).

> **Note**
>
> You will often see dot notation used to reference DataFrame columns. For example, previously we could have done **y** = **df.MEDV.copy()**. This does not work for deleting columns, however; **del df.MEDV** would raise an error.

12. Implement **df.head()** or **df.tail()** to glimpse the data and **len(df)** to verify that number of samples is what we expect. Run the next few cells to see the head, tail, and length of **df**:

```
df.head()
```

	MEDV	CRIM	ZN	INDUS	CHAS	NOX	RM	AGE	DIS	RAD	TAX	PTRATIO	B
0	24.0	0.00632	18.0	2.31	0.0	0.538	6.575	65.2	4.0900	1.0	296.0	15.3	396.90
1	21.6	0.02731	0.0	7.07	0.0	0.469	6.421	78.9	4.9671	2.0	242.0	17.8	396.90
2	34.7	0.02729	0.0	7.07	0.0	0.469	7.185	61.1	4.9671	2.0	242.0	17.8	392.83
3	33.4	0.03237	0.0	2.18	0.0	0.458	6.998	45.8	6.0622	3.0	222.0	18.7	394.63
4	36.2	0.06905	0.0	2.18	0.0	0.458	7.147	54.2	6.0622	3.0	222.0	18.7	396.90

Figure 1.28: Printing the head of the data frame df

```
df.tail()
```

	MEDV	CRIM	ZN	INDUS	CHAS	NOX	RM	AGE	DIS	RAD	TAX	PTRATIO	B
501	22.4	0.06263	0.0	11.93	0.0	0.573	6.593	69.1	2.4786	1.0	273.0	21.0	391.99
502	20.6	0.04527	0.0	11.93	0.0	0.573	6.120	76.7	2.2875	1.0	273.0	21.0	396.90
503	23.9	0.06076	0.0	11.93	0.0	0.573	6.976	91.0	2.1675	1.0	273.0	21.0	396.90
504	22.0	0.10959	0.0	11.93	0.0	0.573	6.794	89.3	2.3889	1.0	273.0	21.0	393.45
505	11.9	0.04741	0.0	11.93	0.0	0.573	6.030	80.8	2.5050	1.0	273.0	21.0	396.90

```
len(df)
```

506

Figure 1.29: Printing the tail of data frame df

Each row is labeled with an index value, as seen in bold on the left side of the table. By default, these are a set of integers starting at 0 and incrementing by one for each row.

13. Printing **df.dtypes** will show the datatype contained within each column. Run the next cell to see the datatypes of each column. For this dataset, we see that every field is a float and therefore most likely a continuous variable, including the target. This means that predicting the target variable is a regression problem.

14. Run **df.isnull()** to clean the dataset as Pandas automatically sets missing data as NaN values. To get the number of NaN values per column, we can do **df.isnull().sum()**:

```
# Identify and NaNs
df.isnull().sum()
```
```
MEDV          0
CRIM          0
ZN            0
INDUS         0
CHAS          0
NOX           0
RM            0
AGE           0
DIS           0
RAD           0
TAX           0
PTRATIO       0
B             0
LSTAT         0
dtype: int64
```

Figure 1.30: Cleaning the dataset by identifying NaN values

df.isnull() returns a Boolean frame of the same length as **df**.

For this dataset, we see there are no **NaN** values, which means we have no immediate work to do in cleaning the data and can move on.

15. Remove some columns by running the cell that contains the following code:

```
for col in ['ZN', 'NOX', 'RAD', 'PTRATIO', 'B']:
    del df[col]
```

This is done to simplify the analysis. We will focus on the remaining columns in more detail.

Data Exploration

Since this is an entirely new dataset that we've never seen before, the first goal here is to understand the data. We've already seen the textual description of the data, which is important for qualitative understanding. We'll now compute a quantitative description.

Exercise 5: Analyzing the Boston Housing Dataset

1. Navigate to **Subtopic B: Data exploration** in the Jupyter Notebook and run the cell containing **df.describe()**:

```
df.describe().T
```

	count	mean	std	min	25%	50%	75%	max
MEDV	506.0	22.532806	9.197104	5.00000	17.025000	21.20000	25.000000	50.0000
CRIM	506.0	3.593761	8.596783	0.00632	0.082045	0.25651	3.647423	88.9762
INDUS	506.0	11.136779	6.860353	0.46000	5.190000	9.69000	18.100000	27.7400
CHAS	506.0	0.069170	0.253994	0.00000	0.000000	0.00000	0.000000	1.0000
RM	506.0	6.284634	0.702617	3.56100	5.885500	6.20850	6.623500	8.7800
AGE	506.0	68.574901	28.148861	2.90000	45.025000	77.50000	94.075000	100.0000
DIS	506.0	3.795043	2.105710	1.12960	2.100175	3.20745	5.188425	12.1265
TAX	506.0	408.237154	168.537116	187.00000	279.000000	330.00000	666.000000	711.0000
LSTAT	506.0	12.653063	7.141062	1.73000	6.950000	11.36000	16.955000	37.9700

Figure 1.31: Computation and output of statistical properties

This computes various properties including the mean, standard deviation, minimum, and maximum for each column. This table gives a high-level idea of how everything is distributed. Note that we have taken the transform of the result by adding a .T to the output; this swaps the rows and columns.

Going forward with the analysis, we will specify a set of columns to focus on.

2. Run the cell where these "focus columns" are defined:

    ```
    cols = ['RM', 'AGE', 'TAX', 'LSTAT', 'MEDV']
    ```

3. Display the aforementioned subset of columns of the DataFrame by running **df[cols].head()**:

```
df[cols].head()
```

	RM	AGE	TAX	LSTAT	MEDV
0	6.575	65.2	296.0	4.98	24.0
1	6.421	78.9	242.0	9.14	21.6
2	7.185	61.1	242.0	4.03	34.7
3	6.998	45.8	222.0	2.94	33.4
4	7.147	54.2	222.0	5.33	36.2

Figure 1.32: Displaying focus columns

As a reminder, let's recall what each of these columns is. From the dataset documentation, we have the following:

```
- RM        average number of rooms per dwelling
   - AGE       proportion of owner-occupied units built prior to 1940
   - TAX       full-value property-tax rate per $10,000
   - LSTAT     % lower status of the population
   - MEDV      Median value of owner-occupied homes in $1000's
```

To look for patterns in this data, we can start by calculating the pairwise correlations using **pd.DataFrame.corr**.

4. Calculate the pairwise correlations for our selected columns by running the cell containing the following code:

    ```
    df[cols].corr()
    ```

	RM	AGE	TAX	LSTAT	MEDV
RM	1.000000	-0.240265	-0.292048	-0.613808	0.695360
AGE	-0.240265	1.000000	0.506456	0.602339	-0.376955
TAX	-0.292048	0.506456	1.000000	0.543993	-0.468536
LSTAT	-0.613808	0.602339	0.543993	1.000000	-0.737663
MEDV	0.695360	-0.376955	-0.468536	-0.737663	1.000000

Figure 1.33: Pairwise calculation of correlation

This resulting table shows the correlation score between each set of values. Large positive scores indicate a strong positive (that is, in the same direction) correlation. As expected, we see maximum values of 1 on the diagonal.

By default, Pandas calculates the standard correlation coefficient for each pair, which is also called the Pearson coefficient. This is defined as the covariance between two variables, divided by the product of their standard deviations:

$$\rho X, Y = \frac{cov(X,Y)}{\rho_x \rho_y}$$

The covariance, in turn, is defned as follows:

$$y = a_0 a + a_1 b + a_2 c + a_3 d$$

Here, n is the number of samples, xi and yi are the individual samples being summed over, and X and Y are the means of each set.

Instead of straining our eyes to look at the preceding table, it's nicer to visualize it with a heatmap. This can be done easily with Seaborn.

5. Run the next cell to initialize the plotting environment, as discussed earlier in the chapter. Then, to create the heatmap, run the cell containing the following code:

```
import matplotlib.pyplot as plt import seaborn as sns
%matplotlib inline
ax = sns.heatmap(df[cols].corr(),
cmap=sns.cubehelix_palette(20, light=0.95,
dark=0.15))
ax.xaxis.tick_top() # move labels to the top
plt.savefig('../figures/lesson-1-boston-housing-corr.png', bbox_
inches='tight', dpi=300)
```

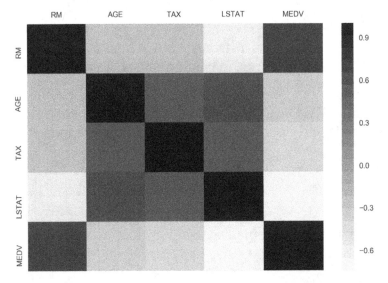

Figure 1.34: Plot of the heat map for all variables

We call **sns.heatmap** and pass the pairwise correlation matrix as input. We use a custom color palette here to override the Seaborn default. The function returns a **matplotlib.axes** object which is referenced by the variable **ax**.

The final figure is then saved as a high resolution PNG to the **figures** folder.

For the final step in our dataset exploration exercise, we'll visualize our data using Seaborn's **pairplot** function.

Visualize the DataFrame using Seaborn's **pairplot** function. Run the cell containing the following code:

```
sns.pairplot(df[cols],
plot_kws={'alpha': 0.6},
diag_kws={'bins': 30})
```

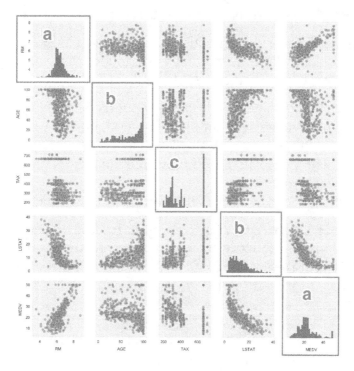

Figure 1.35: Data visualization using Seaborn

Note

Note that unsupervised learning techniques are outside the scope of this book.

Looking at the histograms on the diagonal, we see the following:

a: **RM** and **MEDV** have the closest shape to normal distributions.

b: **AGE** is skewed to the left and **LSTAT** is skewed to the right (this mayseem counterintuitive but skew is defined in terms of where the mean is positioned in relation to the max).

c: For **TAX**, we find a large amount of the distribution is around 700. This is also evident from the scatter plots.

Taking a closer look at the **MEDV** histogram in the bottom right, we actually see something similar to TAX where there is a large upper-limit bin around $50,000. Recall when we did `df.describe()`, the min and max of **MDEV** was 5k and 50k, respectively. This suggests that median house values in the dataset were capped at 50k.

Introduction to Predictive Analytics with Jupyter Notebooks

Continuing our analysis of the Boston housing dataset, we can see that it presents us with a regression problem where we predict a continuous target variable given a set of features. In particular, we'll be predicting the median house value (**MEDV**).

We'll train models that take only one feature as input to make this prediction. This way, the models will be conceptually simple to understand and we can focus more on the technical details of the scikit-learn API. Then, in the next chapter, you'll be more comfortable dealing with the relatively complicated models.

Exercise 6: Applying Linear Models With Seaborn and Scikit-learn

1. Scroll to **Subtopic C: Introduction to predictive analytics** in the Jupyter Notebook and look just above at the pairplot we created in the previous section. In particular, look at the scatter plots in the bottom-left corner:

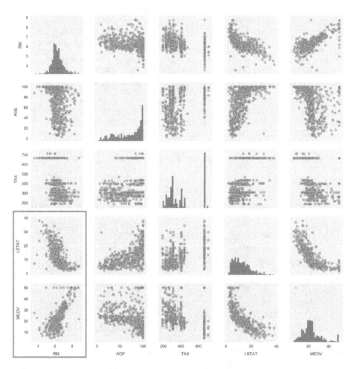

Figure 1.36: Scatter plots for MEDV and LSTAT

Note how the number of rooms per house (**RM**) and the % of the population that is lower class (**LSTAT**) are highly correlated with the median house value (**MDEV**). Let's pose the following question: how well can we predict **MDEV** given these variables?

To help answer this, let's first visualize the relationships using Seaborn. We will draw the scatter plots along with the line of best fit linear models.

2. Draw scatter plots along with the linear models by running the cell that contains the following:

```
fig, ax = plt.subplots(1, 2) sns.regplot('RM', 'MEDV', df, ax=ax[0],
scatter_kws={'alpha': 0.4})) sns.regplot('LSTAT', 'MEDV', df, ax=ax[1],
scatter_kws={'alpha': 0.4}))
```

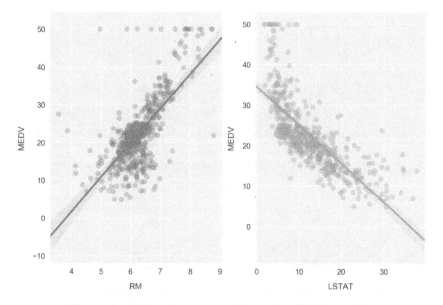

Figure 1.37: Drawing scatter plots using linear models

The line of best fit is calculated by minimizing the ordinary least squares error function, something Seaborn does automatically when we call the **regplot** function. Also note the shaded areas around the lines, which represent 95% confidence intervals.

> **Note**
>
> These 95% confidence intervals are calculated by taking the standard deviation of data in bins perpendicular to the line of best fit, effectively determining the confidence intervals at each point along the line of best fit. In practice, this involves Seaborn bootstrapping the data, a process where new data is created through random sampling with replacement. The number of bootstrapped samples is automatically determined based on the size of the dataset, but can be manually set as well by passing the **n_boot** argument.

3. Plot the residuals using Seaborn by running the cell containing the following:

```
fig, ax = plt.subplots(1, 2)
ax[0] = sns.residplot('RM', 'MEDV', df, ax=ax[0],
scatter_kws={'alpha': 0.4}) ax[0].set_ylabel('MDEV residuals $(y-\
hat{y})$') ax[1] = sns.residplot('LSTAT', 'MEDV', df, ax=ax[1],
scatter_kws={'alpha': 0.4})
ax[1].set_ylabel('')
```

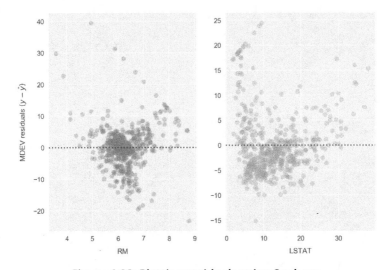

Figure 1.38: Plotting residuals using Seaborn

Each point on these residual plots is the difference between that sample (**y**) and the linear model prediction ($\hat{y}$). Residuals greater than zero are data points that would be underestimated by the model. Likewise, residuals less than zero are data points that would be overestimated by the model.

Patterns in these plots can indicate suboptimal modeling. In each preceding case, we see diagonally arranged scatter points in the positive region. These are caused by the $50,000 cap on **MEDV**. The **RM** data is clustered nicely around 0, which indicates a good fit. On the other hand, **LSTAT** appears to be clustered lower than 0.

4. Define a function using sci-kit learn that calculates the line of best fit and mean squared error, by running the cell that contains the following:

```
def get_mse(df, feature, target='MEDV'): # Get x, y to model
y = df[target].values
x = df[feature].values.reshape(-1,1)
...
...
```

```
error = mean_squared_error(y, y_pred) print('mse = {:.2f}'.format(error))
print()
```

> **Note**
>
> For complete code, refer to the following: https://bit.ly/2JgPZdU

In the **get_mse** function, we first assign the variables **y** and **x** to the target MDEV and the dependent feature, respectively. These are cast as NumPy arrays by calling the **values** attribute. The dependent features array is reshaped to the format expected by scikit-learn; this is only necessary when modeling a one-dimensional feature space. The model is then instantiated and fitted on the data. For linear regression, the fitting consists of computing the model parameters using the ordinary least squares method (minimizing the sum of squared errors for each sample). Finally, after determining the parameters, we predict the target variable and use the results to calculate the **MSE**.

5. Call the **get_mse** function for both **RM** and **LSTAT**, by running the cell containing the following:

```
get_mse(df, 'RM') get_mse(df, 'LSTAT')
```

```
get_mse(df, 'RM')
get_mse df, 'LSTAT'

MEDV ~ RM
model: y = -34.671 + 9.102x
mse = 43.60

MEDV ~ LSTAT
model: y = 34.554 + -0.950x
mse = 38.48
```

Figure 1.39: Calling the get_mse function for RM and LSTAT

Comparing the **MSE**, it turns out the error is slightly lower for **LSTAT**. Looking back to the scatter plots, however, it appears that we might have even better success using a polynomial model for **LSTAT**. In the next activity, we will test this by computing a third-order polynomial model with scikit-learn.

Forgetting about our Boston housing dataset for a minute, consider another real-world situation where you might employ polynomial regression. The following example is modeling weather data. In the following plot, we see temperatures (lines) and precipitations (bars) for Vancouver, BC, Canada:

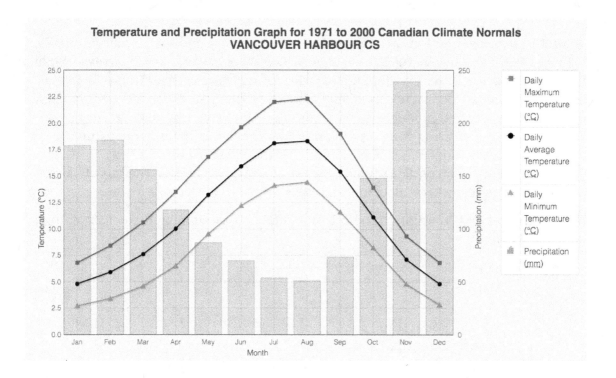

Figure 1.40: Visualizing weather data for Vancouver, Canada

Any of these fields are likely to be fit quite well by a fourth-order polynomial. This would be a very valuable model to have, for example, if you were interested in predicting the temperature or precipitation for a continuous range of dates.

> **Note**
>
> You can find the data source for this here: http://climate.weather.gc.ca/climate_normals/results_e.html?stnID=888.

Activity 1: Building a Third-Order Polynomial Model

Shifting our attention back to the Boston housing dataset, we would like to build a third-order polynomial model to compare against the linear one. Recall the actual problem we are trying to solve: predicting the median house value, given the lower class population percentage. This model could benefit a prospective Boston house purchaser who cares about how much of their community would be lower class.

Our aim is to use scikit-learn to fit a polynomial regression model to predict the median house value (**MEDV**), given the **LSTAT** values. We are hoping to build a model that has a lower mean-squared error (**MSE**). In order to achieve this, the following steps have to be executed:

1. Scroll to the empty cells at the bottom of **Subtopic C** in your Jupyter Notebook. These will be found beneath the linear-model **MSE** calculation cell under the **Activity** heading.

   > **Note**
   >
   > You should fill these empty cells in with code as we complete the activity. You may need to insert new cells as these become filled up; please do so as needed.

2. Pull out our dependent feature from and target variable from **df**.

3. Verify what **x** looks like by printing the first three samples.

4. Transform **x** into "polynomial features" by importing the appropriate transformation tool from scikit-

5. Transform the **LSTAT** feature (as stored in the variable **x**) by running the **fit_transform** method and build the polynomial feature set.

6. Verify what **x_poly** looks like by printing the first few samples.

7. Import the **LinearRegression** class and build our linear classification model the same way as done while calculating the MSE.

8. Extract the coefficients and print the polynomial model.

9. Determine the predicted values for each sample and calculate the residuals.

10. Print some of the residual values.

11. Print the MSE for the third-order polynomial model.

12. Plot the polynomial model along with the samples.

13. Plot the residuals.

> **Note**
>
> The detailed steps along with the solutions are presented in the *Appendix A* (pg. no. 144).

Having successfully modeled the data using a polynomial model, let's finish up this chapter by looking at categorical features. In particular, we are going to build a set of categorical features and use them to explore the dataset in more detail.

Using Categorical Features for Segmentation Analysis

Often, we find datasets where there are a mix of continuous and categorical fields. In such cases, we can learn about our data and find patterns by segmenting the continuous variables with the categorical fields.

As a specific example, imagine you are evaluating the return on investment from an ad campaign. The data you have access to contain measures of some calculated **return on investment** (**ROI**) metric. These values were calculated and recorded daily and you are analyzing data from the previous year. You have been tasked with finding data-driven insights on ways to improve the ad campaign. Looking at the ROI daily time series, you see a weekly oscillation in the data. Segmenting by day of the week, you find the following ROI distributions (where 0 represents the first day of the week and 6 represents the last).

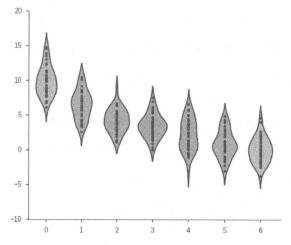

Figure 1.41: A sample violin plot for return on investment

Since we don't have any categorical fields in the Boston housing dataset we are working with, we'll create one by effectively discretizing a continuous field. In our case, this will involve binning the data into "low", "medium", and "high" categories. It's important to note that we are not simply creating a categorical data field to illustrate the data analysis concepts in this section. As will be seen, doing this can reveal insights from the data that would otherwise be difficult to notice or altogether unavailable.

Exercise 7: Creating Categorical Fields From Continuous Variables and Make Segmented Visualizations

1. Scroll up to the pairplot in the Jupyter Notebook where we compared **MEDV**, **LSTAT**, **TAX**, **AGE**, and **RM**:

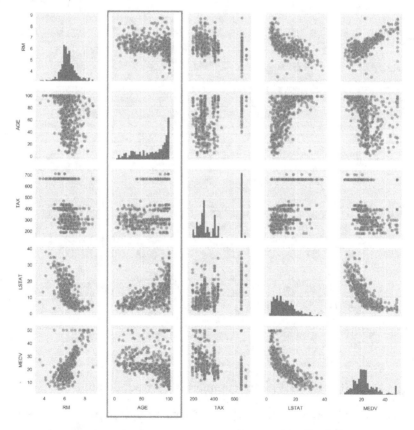

Figure 1.42: A comparison of plots for MEDV, LSTAT, TAX, AGE, and RM

Take a look at the panels containing **AGE**. As a reminder, this feature is defined as the proportion of *owner-occupied units built prior to 1940*. We are going to convert this feature to a categorical variable. Once it's been converted, we'll be able to replot this figure with each panel segmented by color according to the age category.

2. Scroll down to **Subtopic D: Building and exploring categorical features** and click into the first cell. Type and execute the following to plot the **AGE** cumulative distribution:

```
sns.distplot(df.AGE.values, bins=100,
hist_kws={'cumulative': True}, kde_kws={'lw': 0})
plt.xlabel('AGE') plt.ylabel('CDF') plt.axhline(0.33, color='red') plt.
axhline(0.66, color='red')
plt.xlim(0, df.AGE.max());
```

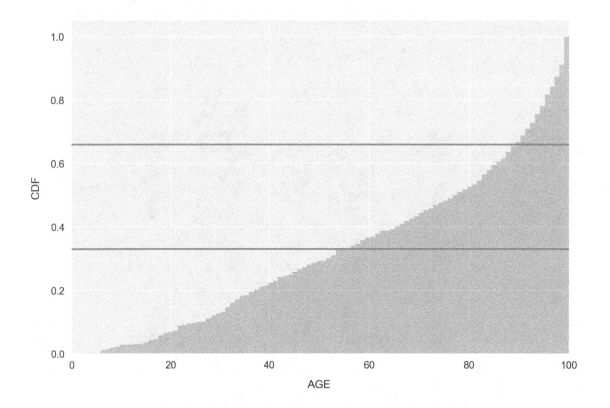

Figure 1.43: Plot for cumulative distribution of AGE

Note that we set **kde_kws={'lw': 0}** in order to bypass plotting the kernel density estimate in the preceding figure.

Looking at the plot, there are very few samples with low **AGE**, whereas there are far more with a very large **AGE**. This is indicated by the steepness of the distribution on the far right-hand side.

The red lines indicate 1/3 and 2/3 points in the distribution. Looking at the places where our distribution intercepts these horizontal lines, we can see that only about 33% of the samples have **AGE** less than 55 and 33% of the samples have **AGE** greater than 90! In other words, a third of the housing communities have less than 55% of homes built prior to 1940. These would be considered relatively new communities. On the other end of the spectrum, another third of the housing communities have over 90% of homes built prior to 1940. These would be considered very old. We'll use the places where the red horizontal lines intercept the distribution as a guide to split the feature into categories: **Relatively New**, **Relatively Old**, and **Very Old**.

3. Create a new categorical feature and set the segmentation points by running the following code:

```
def get_age_category(x): if x < 50:
return 'Relatively New' elif 50 <= x < 85:
return 'Relatively Old' else:
return 'Very Old'

df['AGE_category'] = df.AGE.apply(get_age_category)
```

Here, we are using the very handy Pandas method apply, which applies a function to a given column or set of columns. The function being applied, in this case **get_age_category**, should take one argument representing a row of data and return one value for the new column. In this case, the row of data being passed is just a single value, the **AGE** of the sample.

> **Note**
>
> The apply method is great because it can solve a variety of problems and allows for easily readable code. Often though, vectorized methods such as **pd.Series.str** can accomplish the same thing much faster. Therefore, it's advised to avoid using it if possible, especially when working with large datasets. We'll see some examples of vectorized methods in the upcoming chapter.

4. Verify the number of samples we've grouped into each age category by typing `df.groupby('AGE_category').size()` into a new cell and running it:

```
# Check the segmented counts
df.groupby('AGE_category').size()
```

```
AGE_category
Relatively New    147
Relatively Old    149
Very Old          210
dtype: int64
```

Figure 1.44: Verifying the grouping of variables

Looking at the result, it can be seen that two class sizes are fairly equal, and the **Very Old** group is about 40% larger. We are interested in keeping the classes comparable in size, so that each is well-represented and it's straightforward to make inferences from the analysis.

> **Note**
>
> It may not always be possible to assign samples into classes evenly, and in real-world situations, it's very common to find highly imbalanced classes. In such cases, it's important to keep in mind that it will be difficult to make statistically significant claims with respect to the under-represented class. Predictive analytics with imbalanced classes can be particularly difficult. The following blog post offers an excellent summary on methods for handling imbalanced classes when doing machine learning: https://svds.com/learning-imbalanced-classes/.

Let's see how the target variable is distributed when segmented by our new feature **AGE_category**.

5. Construct a violin plot by running the following code:

```
sns.violinplot(x='MEDV', y='AGE_category', data=df, order=['Relatively
New', 'Relatively Old',
'Very Old']);
```

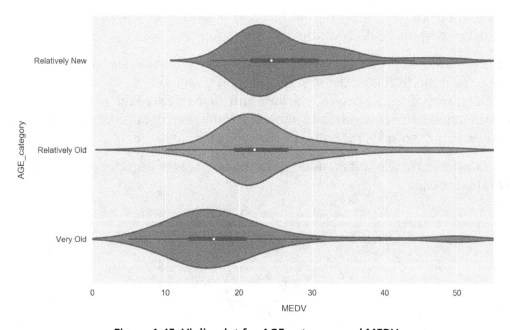

Figure 1.45: Violin plot for AGE_category and MEDV

The violin plot shows a kernel density estimate of the median house value distribution for each age category. We see that they all resemble a normal distribution. The Very Old group contains the lowest median house value samples and has a relatively large width, whereas the other groups are more tightly centered around their average. The young group is skewed to the high end, which is evident from the enlarged right half and position of the white dot in the thick black line within the body of the distribution.

This white dot represents the mean and the thick black line spans roughly 50% of the population (it fills to the first quantile on either side of the white dot). The thin black line represents boxplot whiskers and spans 95% of the population. This inner visualization can be modified to show the individual data points instead by passing `inner='point'` to `sns.violinplot()`. Let's do that now.

6. Re-construct the violin plot adding the `inner='point'` argument to the **sns. violinplot** call:

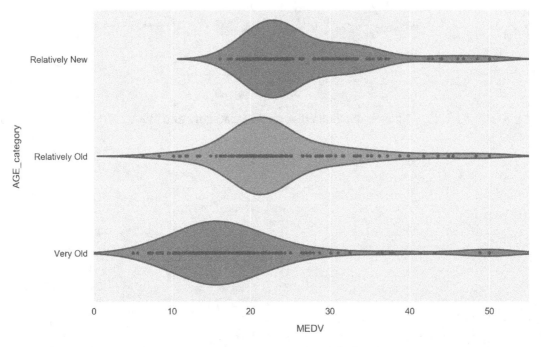

Figure 1.46: Violin plot for AGE_category and MEDV with the inner = 'point' argument

It's good to make plots like this for test purposes in order to see how the underlying data connects to the visual. We can see, for example, how there are no median house values lower than roughly $16,000 for the **Relatively New** segment, and therefore the distribution tail actually contains no data. Due to the small size of our dataset (only about 500 rows), we can see this is the case for each segment.

7. Re-construct the pairplot from earlier, but now include color labels for each **AGE** category. This is done by simply passing the **hue** argument, as follows:

```
cols = ['RM', 'AGE', 'TAX', 'LSTAT', 'MEDV', 'AGE_
category']
sns.pairplot(df[cols], hue='AGE_category',
hue_order=['Relatively New', 'Relatively Old',
'Very Old'],
plot_kws={'alpha': 0.5}, diag_kws={'bins':
30});
```

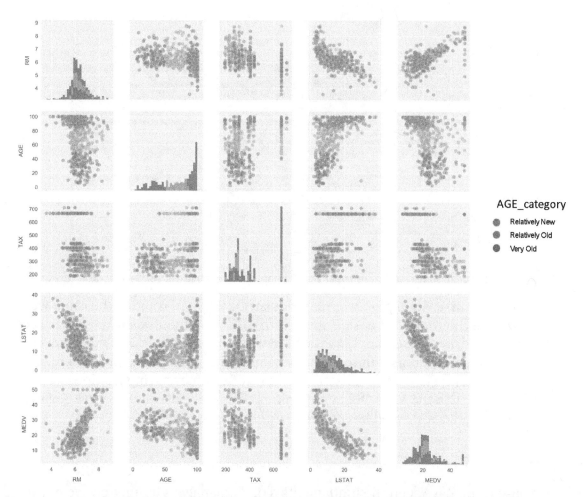

Figure 1.47: Re-constructing pairplot for all variables using color labels for AGE

Looking at the histograms, the underlying distributions of each segment appear similar for **RM** and **TAX**. The **LSTAT** distributions, on the other hand, look more distinct. We can focus on them in more detail by again using a violin plot.

8. Re-construct a violin plot comparing the LSTAT distributions for each `AGE_category` segment:

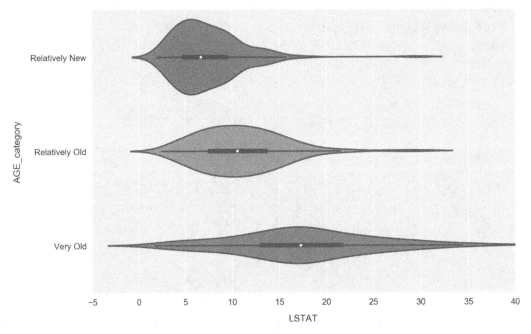

Figure 1.48: Re-constructed violin plots for comparing LSTAT distributions for the AGE_category

Unlike the **MEDV** violin plot, where each distribution had roughly the same width, here we see the width increasing along with **AGE**. Communities with primarily old houses (the **Very Old** segment) contain anywhere from very few to many lower class residents, whereas **Relatively New** communities are much more likely to be predominantly higher class, with over 95% of samples having less lower class percentages than the **Very Old** communities. This makes sense, because **Relatively New** neighborhoods would be more expensive.

Summary

In this chapter, you have seen the fundamentals of data analysis in Jupyter. We began with usage instructions and features of Jupyter such as magic functions and tab completion. Then, transitioning to data-science-specific material, we introduced the most important libraries for data science with Python.

In the latter half of the chapter, we ran an exploratory analysis in a live Jupyter Notebook. Here, we used visual assists such as scatter plots, histograms, and violin plots to deepen our understanding of the data. We also performed simple predictive modeling, a topic which will be the focus of the following chapter in this book.

In the next chapter, we will discuss how to approach predictive analytics, what things to consider when preparing the data for modeling, and how to implement and compare a variety of models using Jupyter Notebooks.

Data Cleaning
and Advanced
Machine Learning

Learning Objectives

By the end of this chapter, you will be able to:

- Plan a machine learning classification strategy

- Preprocess data to prepare it for machine learning

- Train classification models

- Use validation curves to tune model parameters

- Use dimensionality reduction to enhance model performance

In this chapter, you will learn data preprocessing and machine learning by completing several practical exercises.

Introduction

Consider a small food-delivery business that is looking to optimize their product. An analyst might look at the appropriate data and determine what type of food people are enjoying most. Perhaps they find a large amount of people are ordering the spiciest food options, indicating the business might be losing out on customers who desire something even more spicy. This is quite basic, or as some might say, "vanilla" analytics.

In a separate task, the analyst could employ predictive analytics by modeling the order volumes over time. With enough data, they could predict the future order volumes and therefore guide the restaurant as to how many staff are required each day. This model could take factors such as the weather into account to make the best predictions. For instance, a heavy rainstorm could be an indicator to staff more delivery personnel to make up for slow travel times. With historical weather data, that type of signal could be encoded into the model. This prediction model would save a business the time of having to consider these problems manually, and money by keeping customers happy and thereby increasing customer retention.

The goal of data analytics in general is to uncover actionable insights that result in positive business outcomes. In the case of predictive analytics, the aim is to do this by determining the most likely future outcome of a target, based on previous trends and patterns.

The benefits of predictive analytics are not restricted to big technology companies. Any business can find ways to benefit from machine learning, given the right data.

Companies all around the world are collecting massive amounts of data and using predictive analytics to cut costs and increase profits. Some of the most prevalent examples of this are from the technology giants Google, Facebook, and Amazon, who utilize big data on a huge scale. For example, Google and Facebook serve you personalized ads based on predictive algorithms that guess what you are most likely to click on. Similarly, Amazon recommends personalized products that you are most likely to buy, given your previous purchases.

Modern predictive analytics is done with machine learning, where computer models are trained to learn patterns from data. As we saw briefly in the previous chapter, software such as scikit-learn can be used with Jupyter Notebooks to efficiently build and test machine learning models. As we will continue to see, Jupyter Notebooks are an ideal environment for doing this type of work, as we can perform ad-hoc testing and analysis, and easily save the results for reference later.

In this chapter, we will again take a hands-on approach by running through various examples and activities in a Jupyter Notebook. Where we saw a couple of examples of machine learning in the previous chapter, here we'll take a much slower and more thoughtful approach. Using an employee retention problem as our overarching example for the chapter, we will discuss how to approach predictive analytics, what things to consider when preparing the data for modeling, and how to implement and compare a variety of models using Jupyter Notebooks.

Preparing to Train a Predictive Model

Here, we will cover the preparation required to train a predictive model. Although not as technically glamorous as training the models themselves, this step should not be taken lightly. It's very important to ensure you have a good plan before proceeding with the details of building and training a reliable model. Furthermore, once you've decided on the right plan, there are technical steps in preparing the data for modeling that should not be overlooked.

> **Note**
>
> We must be careful not to go so deep into the weeds of technical tasks that we lose sight of the goal. Technical tasks include things that require programming skills, for example, constructing visualizations, querying databases, and validating predictive models. It's easy to spend hours trying to implement a specific feature or get the plots looking just right. Doing this sort of thing is certainly beneficial to our programming skills, but we should not forget to ask ourselves if it's really worth our time with respect to the current project.

Also, keep in mind that Jupyter Notebooks are particularly well-suited for this step, as we can use them to document our plan, for example, by writing rough notes about the data or a list of models we are interested in training. Before starting to train models, its good practice to even take this a step further and write out a well- structured plan to follow. Not only will this help you stay on track as you build and test the models, but it will allow others to understand what you're doing when they see your work.

After discussing the preparation, we will also cover another step in preparing to train the predictive model, which is cleaning the dataset. This is another thing that Jupyter Notebooks are well-suited for, as they offer an ideal testing ground for performing dataset transformations and keeping track of the exact changes. The data transformations required for cleaning raw data can quickly become intricate and convoluted; therefore, it's important to keep track of your work. As discussed in the first chapter, tools other than Jupyter Notebooks just don't offer very good options for doing this efficiently.

Before we progress to the next section, let's pause and think about these ideas in the context of a real-life example.

Consider the following situation:

You are hired by an online video game marketplace who want to increase the conversion rate of people visiting their site. They ask you to use predictive analytics to determine what genre of game the user will like, so they can display specialized content that will encourage the user to make a purchase. They want to do this without having to ask the customer their preference of game genre.

Is this a problem that can be solved? What type of data would be required? What would be the business implications?

To address this challenge, we could consider making the prediction based on users' browsing cookies. For example, if they have a cookie from previously visiting a World of Warcraft website, this would act as an indicator that they like role playing games.

Another valuable piece of data would be a history of the games that user has previously bought in the marketplace. This could be the target variable in a machine learning algorithm, for example, a model that could predict which games the user would be interested in, based on the type of cookies in their browsing session. An alternate target variable could be constructed by setting up a survey in the marketplace to collect data on user preferences.

In terms of the business implications, being able to accurately predict the genre of game is very important to the success of the campaign. In fact, getting the prediction wrong is doubly problematic: not only do we miss out on the opportunity to target users, but we may end up showing users content that would be negatively perceived. This could lead to more people leaving the site and fewer sales.

Determining a Plan for Predictive Analytics

When formulating a plan for doing predictive modeling, one should start by considering stakeholder needs. A perfect model will be useless if it doesn't solve a relevant problem. Planning a strategy around business needs ensures that a successful model will lead to actionable insights.

Although it may be possible in principle to solve many business problems, the ability to deliver the solution will always depend on the availability of the necessary data. Therefore, it's important to consider the business needs in the context of the available data sources. When data is plentiful, this will have little effect, but as the amount of available data becomes smaller, so too does the scope of problems that can be solved.

These ideas can be formed into a standard process for determining a predictive analytics plan, which goes as follows:

1. **Look at the available data** to understand the range of realistically solvable business problems. At this stage, it might be too early to think about the exact problems that can be solved. Make sure you understand the data fields available and the timeframes they apply to.

2. **Determine the business needs** by speaking with key stakeholders. Seek out a problem where the solution will lead to actionable business decisions.

3. **Assess the data for suitability** by considering the availability of a sufficiently diverse and large feature space. Also, take into account the condition of the data: are there large chunks of missing values for certain variables or time ranges?

Steps 2 and 3 should be repeated until a realistic plan has taken shape. At this point, you will already have a good idea of what the model input will be and what you might expect as output.

Once you've identified a problem that can be solved with machine learning, along with the appropriate data sources, we should answer the following questions to lay a framework for the project. Doing this will help us determine which types of machine learning models we can use to solve the problem. The following image provides an overview of the choices available depending on the type of data:

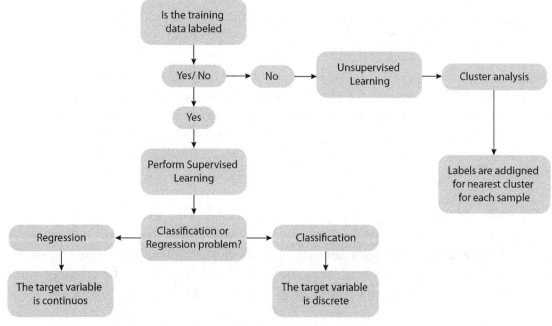

Figure 2.1: A flow chart for machine learning strategy based on the type of data

The above image describes the path you can choose depending of the type of data: labeled or unlabeled.

As can be seen, either one can chose supervised or unsupervised learning. Supervised learning comprises either classification or regression problem. In regression, variables are continuous; for example, the amount of rainfall. In regression, the variables are discrete and we predict class labels. Simplest type of classification problem is binary; for example, will it rain today? (yes/no)

For unsupervised learning, cluster analysis is a commonly used method. Here, labels are assigned to the nearest cluster for each sample.

However, not only the type but also the size and origin of data sources would be a factor while deciding on machine learning strategy. Specifically, following points should be note:

- The size of data in terms of the width (no. of columns) and height (no. of rows) should be considered before apply a machine learning algorithm.

- Certain algorithms are better at handling certain features than the others.

- General, the larger the dataset, the better in terms of accuracy. However, this can be time consuming

- One can reduce time by using dimensionality reduction techniques.

- For multiple data sources, one can consider merging them in a single table.

- If this cannot be done, we can train models for each and consider an ensemble average for final prediction.

An example where we may want to do this is with various sets of times series data on different scales. Consider we have the following data sources: a table with the AAPL stock closing prices on a daily time scale and iPhone sales data on a monthly time scale. We could merge the data by adding the monthly sales data to each sample in the daily time scale table, or grouping the daily data by month, but it might be better to build two models, one for each dataset, and use a combination of the results from each in the final prediction model.

Data preprocessing has a huge impact on machine learning. Like the saying "you are what you eat," the model's performance is a direct reflection of the data it's trained on. Many models depend on the data being transformed so that the continuous feature values have comparable limits. Similarly, categorical features should be encoded into numerical values. Although important, these steps are relatively simple and do not take very long.

The aspect of preprocessing that usually takes the longest is cleaning up messy data. Some estimates suggest that data scientists spend around two thirds of their work time cleaning and organizing datasets:

Figure 2.2: A pie chart distribution of the time spend on different data tasks

To know more about the preprocessing stage, refer to: https://www.forbes.com/sites/gilpress/2016/03/23/data- preparation-most-time-consuming-least-enjoyable-data-science-task-survey-says/2/#17c66c7e1492.

Another thing to consider is the size of the datasets being used by many data scientists. As the dataset size increases, the prevalence of messy data increases as well, along with the difficulty in cleaning it.

Simply dropping the missing data is usually not the best option, because it's hard to justify throwing away samples where most of the fields have values. In doing so, we could lose valuable information that may hurt final model performance.

> **Note**
>
> In this exercise, we practice preprocessing the data by creating two DataFrames, and performing an inner merge and outer merge on the DataFrames and remove the null (**NaN**) values.

The steps involved in data preprocessing can be grouped as follows:

- **Merging data** sets on common fields to bring all data into a single table
- **Feature engineering** to improve the quality of data, for example, the use of dimensionality reduction techniques to build new features

- **Cleaning the data** by dealing with duplicate rows, incorrect or missing values, and other issues that arise

- **Building the training data sets** by standardizing or normalizing the required data and splitting it into training and testing sets

Let's explore some of the tools and methods for doing the preprocessing.

Exercise 8: Explore Data Preprocessing Tools and Methods

1. Start the **NotebookApp** from the project directory by executing **jupyter notebook**. Navigate to the **Lesson-2** directory and open up the **lesson- 2-workbook.ipynb** file. Find the cell near the top where the packages are loaded, and run it.

    We are going to start by showing off some basic tools from Pandas and sci-kit learn. Then, we'll take a deeper dive into methods for rebuilding missing data.

2. Scroll down to **Subtopic B: Preparing data for machine learning** and run the cell containing **pd.merge?** to display the docstring for the merge function in the notebook:

```
Signature: pd.merge(left, right, how='inner', on=None, left_on=None, right_on=None, left_
index=False, right_index=False, sort=False, suffixes=('_x', '_y'), copy=True, indicator=F
alse)
Docstring:
Merge DataFrame objects by performing a database-style join operation by
columns or indexes.

If joining columns on columns, the DataFrame indexes *will be
ignored*. Otherwise if joining indexes on indexes or indexes on a column or
columns, the index will be passed on.

Parameters
----------
left : DataFrame
right : DataFrame
how : {'left', 'right', 'outer', 'inner'}, default 'inner'
    * left: use only keys from left frame, similar to a SQL left outer join;
      preserve key order
    * right: use only keys from right frame, similar to a SQL right outer join;
      preserve key order
    * outer: use union of keys from both frames, similar to a SQL full outer
      join; sort keys lexicographically
    * inner: use intersection of keys from both frames, similar to a SQL inner
      join; preserve the order of the left keys
on : label or list
    Field names to join on. Must be found in both DataFrames. If on is
    None and not merging on indexes, then it merges on the intersection of
    the columns by default.
left_on : label or list, or array-like
    Field names to join on in left DataFrame. Can be a vector or list of
    vectors of the length of the DataFrame to use a particular vector as
    the join key instead of columns
```

Figure 2.3: Docstring for the merge function

As we can see, the function accepts a left and right DataFrame to merge. You can specify one or more columns to group on as well as how they are grouped, that is, to use the left, right, outer, or inner sets of values. Let's see an example of this in use.

3. Exit the help popup and run the cell containing the following sample DataFrames:

```
df_1 = pd.DataFrame({'product': ['red shirt', 'red shirt', 'red shirt',
'white dress'],\n",
'price': [49.33, 49.33, 32.49,
199.99]})\n",
df_2 = pd.DataFrame({'product': ['red shirt', 'blue pants', 'white
tuxedo', 'white dress'],\n",
'in_stock': [True, True, False,
False]})
```

Here, we will build two simple DataFrames from scratch. As can be seen, they contain a **product** column with some shared entries.

4. Run the next cell to perform the inner merge:

```
# Inner merge

df = pd.merge(left=df_1, right=df_2, on='product', how='inner')
df
```

	price	product	in_stock
0	49.33	red shirt	True
1	49.33	red shirt	True
2	32.49	red shirt	True
3	199.99	white dress	False

Figure 2.3: Inner merge of columns

Note how only the shared items, **red shirt** and **white dress**, are included. To include all entries from both tables, we can do an outer merge instead. Let's do this now.

5. Run the next cell to perform an outer merge:

```
# Outer merge

df = pd.merge(left=df_1, right=df_2, on='product', how='outer')
df
```

	price	product	in_stock
0	49.33	red shirt	True
1	49.33	red shirt	True
2	32.49	red shirt	True
3	199.99	white dress	False
4	NaN	blue pants	True
5	NaN	white tuxedo	False

Figure 2.4: Outer merge of columns

This returns all of the data from each table where missing values have been labeled with **NaN**.

```
a = float('nan')
```

```
bool(a)
```
True

```
a == float('nan')
```
False

```
a is float('nan')
```
False

```
np.isnan(a)
```
True

Figure 2.5: Code for using NumPy to test for quality

You may have noticed that our most recently merged table has duplicated data in the first few rows. This will be addressed in the next step.

6. Run the cell containing **df.drop_duplicates()** to return a version of the DataFrame with no duplicate rows:

	price	product	in_stock
0	49.33	red shirt	True
2	32.49	red shirt	True
3	199.99	white dress	False
4	NaN	blue pants	True
5	NaN	white tuxedo	False

df.drop_duplicates()

Figure 2.6: Table with dropped duplicate rows

This is the easiest and "standard" way to drop duplicate rows. To apply these changes to **df**, we can either set **inplace=True** or do something like **df = df.drop_duplicated()**. Let's see another method, which uses masking to select or drop duplicate rows.

7. Run the cell containing **df.duplicated()** to print the True/False series, marking duplicate rows:

```
df.duplicated()
0    False
1     True
2    False
3    False
4    False
5    False
dtype: bool
```

Figure 2.7: Printing True/False values for duplicate rows

8. Sum the result to determine how many rows have been duplicated by running the following code:

```
df.duplicated().sum()
```

```
1
```

```
df[df.duplicated()]
```

	price	product	in_stock
1	49.33	red shirt	True

Figure 2.8: Summing the result to check the number of duplicate rows

9. Run the following code and convince yourself the output is the same as that from **df.drop_duplicates():**

```
df[~df.duplicated()]
```

```
df[~df.duplicated()]
```

	price	product	in_stock
0	49.33	red shirt	True
2	32.49	red shirt	True
3	199.99	white dress	False
4	NaN	blue pants	True
5	NaN	white tuxedo	False

Figure 2.9: Output from the df.[~df.duplicated()] function

10. Run the cell containing the following code to drop duplicates from a subset of the full DataFrame:

```
df[~df['product'].duplicated()]
```

```
df[~df['product'].duplicated()]
```

	price	product	in_stock
0	49.33	red shirt	True
3	199.99	white dress	False
4	NaN	blue pants	True
5	NaN	white tuxedo	False

Figure 2.10: Output after dropping duplicates

Here, we are doing the following things:

creating a mask (a True/False series) for the product row, where duplicates are marked with **True**;

using the tilde (~) to take the opposite of that mask, so that duplicates are instead marked with False and everything else is **True**;

using that mask to filter out the **False** rows of **df**, which correspond to the duplicated products.

As expected, we now see that only the first **red shirt** row remains, as the duplicate product rows have been removed.

In order to proceed with the exercise, let's replace **df** with a deduplicated version of itself. This can be done by running **drop_duplicates** and passing the parameter **inplace=True**.

11. Deduplicate the DataFrame and save the result by running the cell containing the following code:

```
df.drop_duplicates(inplace=True)
```

Continuing on to other preprocessing methods, let's ignore the duplicated rows and first deal with the missing data. This is necessary because models cannot be trained on incomplete samples. Using the missing price data for blue pants and white tuxedo as an example, let's show some different options for handling **NaN** values.

12. Drop rows, especially if your **NaN** samples are missing data, by running the cell containing **df.dropna()**:

```
# Drop the incomplete rows

df.dropna()
```

	price	product	in_stock
0	49.33	red shirt	True
2	32.49	red shirt	True
3	199.99	white dress	False

Figure 2.11: Output after dropping incomplete rows

13. Drop entire columns that have most values missing for a feature. Do this by running the cell containing the same method as before, but this time with the axes parameter passed to indicate columns instead of rows:

```
# Drop the incomplete columns

df.dropna(axis=1)
```

	product	in_stock
0	red shirt	True
2	red shirt	True
3	white dress	False
4	blue pants	True
5	white tuxedo	False

Figure 2.12: Output after dropping entire columns with missing values for a feature

Simply dropping the **NaN** values is usually not the best option, because losing data is never good, especially if only a small fraction of the sample values is missing. Pandas offers a method for filling in **NaN** entries in a variety of different ways, some of which we'll illustrate now.

14. Run the cell containing **df.fillna?** to print the docstring for the Pandas **NaN-fill** method:

```
Signature: df.fillna(value=None, method=None, axis=None, inplace=False, limit=None, downc
ast=None, **kwargs)
Docstring:
Fill NA/NaN values using the specified method

Parameters
----------
value : scalar, dict, Series, or DataFrame
    Value to use to fill holes (e.g. 0), alternately a
    dict/Series/DataFrame of values specifying which value to use for
    each index (for a Series) or column (for a DataFrame). (values not
    in the dict/Series/DataFrame will not be filled). This value cannot
    be a list.
method : {'backfill', 'bfill', 'pad', 'ffill', None}, default None
    Method to use for filling holes in reindexed Series
    pad / ffill: propagate last valid observation forward to next valid
    backfill / bfill: use NEXT valid observation to fill gap
axis : {0 or 'index', 1 or 'columns'}
inplace : boolean, default False
    If True, fill in place. Note: this will modify any
    other views on this object, (e.g. a no-copy slice for a column in a
    DataFrame).
```

Figure 2.13: Docstring for the NaN-fill method

Note the options for the value parameter; this could be, for example, a single value or a dictionary/series type map based on index. Alternatively, we can leave the value as **None** and pass a **fill** method instead. We'll see examples of each in this chapter.

15. Fill in the missing data with the average product price by running the cell containing the following code:

```
df.fillna(value=df.price.mean())
```

```
# Fill with the average

df.fillna(value=df.price.mean())
```

	price	product	in_stock
0	49.330000	red shirt	True
2	32.490000	red shirt	True
3	199.990000	white dress	False
4	93.936667	blue pants	True
5	93.936667	white tuxedo	False

Figure 2.14: Output after filling missing data with average product price

16. Fill in the missing data using the pad method by running the cell containing the following code instead:

```
df.fillna(method='pad')
```

```
# Fill with the previous value in that column

df.fillna(method='pad')
```

	price	product	in_stock
0	49.33	red shirt	True
2	32.49	red shirt	True
3	199.99	white dress	False
4	199.99	blue pants	True
5	199.99	white tuxedo	False

Figure 2.15: Output after filling data using the pad method

Notice how the **white dress** price was used to pad the missing values below it.

To conclude this exercise, we will prepare our simple table to be used for training a machine learning algorithm. Don't worry, we won't actually try to train any models on such a small dataset! We start this process by encoding the class labels for the categorical data.

17. Run the first cell in the **Building training data sets** section to add another column of data representing the average product ratings before encoding the labels:

```
df = df.fillna(value=df.price.mean())
ratings = ['low', 'medium', 'high']
np.random.seed(2)
df['rating'] = np.random.choice(ratings, len(df))
df
```

	price	product	in_stock	rating
0	49.330000	red shirt	True	low
2	32.490000	red shirt	True	medium
3	199.990000	white dress	False	low
4	93.936667	blue pants	True	high
5	93.936667	white tuxedo	False	high

Figure 2.16: Output after adding the rating column

Considering we want to use this table to train a predictive model, we should first think about changing all the variables to numeric types.

18. Convert the handle **in_stock.**, which is a Boolean list, to numeric values; for example, **0** and **1**. This should be done before using it to train a predictive model. This can be done in many ways, for example, by running the cell containing the following code:

```
df.in_stock = df.in_stock.map({False: 0, True: 1})
```

```
# Convert in_stock to binary

df.in_stock = df.in_stock.map({False: 0, True: 1})
df
```

	price	product	in_stock	rating
0	49.330000	red shirt	1	low
2	32.490000	red shirt	1	medium
3	199.990000	white dress	0	low
4	93.936667	blue pants	1	high
5	93.936667	white tuxedo	0	high

Figure 2.17: Output after converting in_stock to binary

19. Run the cell containing the following code to map class labels to integers at a higher level. We use sci-kit learn's **LabelEncoder** for this purpose:

```
from sklearn.preprocessing import LabelEncoder rating_encoder =
LabelEncoder()
_df = df.copy()
_df.rating = rating_encoder.fit_transform(df.rating)
_df
```

```
# Encode labels

from sklearn.preprocessing import LabelEncoder
rating_encoder = LabelEncoder()
_df = df.copy()
_df.rating = rating_encoder.fit_transform(df.rating)
_df
```

	price	product	in_stock	rating
0	49.330000	red shirt	1	1
2	32.490000	red shirt	1	2
3	199.990000	white dress	0	1
4	93.936667	blue pants	1	0
5	93.936667	white tuxedo	0	0

Figure 2.18: Output after mapping class labels to integers

This might bring to mind the preprocessing we did in the previous chapter, when building the polynomial model. Here, we instantiate a label encoder and then "train" it and "transform" our data using the **fit_transform** method. We apply the result to a copy of our DataFrame, **_df**.

20. Re-convert the features using the class we reference with the variable **rating_encoder**, by running **rating_encoder.inverse_ transform(df.rating)**:

```
# Convert back if needed

rating_encoder.inverse_transform(_df.rating)
```

```
array(['low', 'medium', 'low', 'high', 'high'], dtype=object)
```

Figure 2.19: Output after performing inverse transform

You may notice a problem here. We are working with a so-called "ordinal" feature, where there's an inherent order to the labels. In this case, we should expect that a rating of "low" would be encoded with a 0 and a rating of "high" would be encoded with a 2. However, this is not the result we see. In order to achieve proper ordinal label encoding, we should again use map, and build the dictionary ourselves.

21. Encode the ordinal labels properly by running the cell containing the following code:

```
ordinal_map = {rating: index for index, rating in enumerate(['low',
'medium', 'high'])}
```

```
print(ordinal_map)
df.rating = df.rating.map(ordinal_map)
```

```
# Encode ordinal labels

ordinal_map = {rating: index for index, rating in enumerate(['low', 'medium', 'high'])}
print(ordinal_map)

df.rating = df.rating.map(ordinal_map)
df
```

```
{'low': 0, 'high': 2, 'medium': 1}
```

	price	product	in_stock	rating
0	49.330000	red shirt	1	0
2	32.490000	red shirt	1	1
3	199.990000	white dress	0	0
4	93.936667	blue pants	1	2
5	93.936667	white tuxedo	0	2

Figure 2.20: Output after encoding ordinal labels

We first create the mapping dictionary. This is done using a dictionary comprehension and enumeration, but looking at the result, we see that it could just as easily be defined manually instead. Then, as done earlier for the **in_stock** column, we apply the dictionary mapping to the feature. Looking at the result, we see that rating now makes more sense than before, where **low** is labeled with **0**, **medium** with **1**, and **high** with **2**.

Now that you've discussed ordinal features, let's touch on another type called nominal features. These are fields with no inherent order, and in our case, we see that **product** is a perfect example.

Most scikit-learn models can be trained on data like this, where we have strings instead of integer-encoded labels. In this situation, the necessary conversions are done under the hood. However, this may not be the case for all models in scikit-learn, or other machine learning and deep learning libraries. Therefore, it's good practice to encode these ourselves during preprocessing.

22. Convert the class labels from strings to numerical values by running the cell containing the following code:

```
df = pd.get_dummies(df)
```

The final DataFrame then looks as follows:

```
# Convert back if needed

rating_encoder.inverse_transform(_df.rating)

array(['low', 'medium', 'low', 'high', 'high'], dtype=object)
```

Figure 2.21: Final DataFrame

Here, we see the result of one-hot encoding: the **product** column has been split into 4, one for each unique value. Within each column, we find either a **1** or **0** representing whether that row contains the particular value or product.

Moving on and ignoring any data scaling (which should usually be done), the final step is to split the data into training and test sets to use for machine learning. This can be done using scikit-learn's **train_test_split**. Let's assume we are going to try to predict whether an item is in stock, given the other feature values.

> **Note**
>
> When we call the values attribute in the preceding code, we are converting the Pandas series (that is, the DataFrame column) into a NumPy array. This is good practice because it strips out unnecessary information from the series object, such as the index and name.

23. Split the data into training and test sets by running the cell containing the following code:

```
features = ['price', 'rating', 'product_blue pants', 'product_red shirt',
'product_white dress', 'product_white tuxedo']
X = df[features].values target = 'in_stock'
y = df[target].values
from sklearn.model_selection import train_test_split X_train, X_test, y_
train, y_test = \
train_test_split(X, y, test_size=0.3)
```

```
print('            shape')
print('----------------')
print('X_train', X_train.shape)
print('X_test ', X_test.shape)
print('y_train', y_train.shape)
print('y_test ', y_test.shape)
```

```
            shape
----------------
X_train (3, 6)
X_test  (2, 6)
y_train (3,)
y_test  (2,)
```

Figure 2.22: Splitting data intro training and test sets

Here, we are selecting subsets of the data and feeding them into the **train_test_split** function. This function has four outputs, which are unpacked into the training and testing splits for features (**X**) and the target (**y**).

Observe the shape of the output data, where the test set has roughly 30% of the samples and the training set has roughly 70%.

We'll see similar code blocks later, when preparing real data to use for training predictive models.

This concludes the training exercise on cleaning data for use in machine learning applications. Let's take a minute to note how effective our Jupyter Notebook was for testing various methods of transforming the data, and ultimately documenting the pipeline we decided upon. This could easily be applied to an updated version of the data by altering only specific cells of code, prior to processing. Also, should we desire any changes to the processing, these can easily be tested in the notebook, and specific cells may be changed to accommodate the alterations. The best way to achieve this would probably be to copy the notebook over to a new file, so that we can always keep a copy of the original analysis for reference.

Moving on to an activity, we'll now apply the concepts from this section to a large dataset as we prepare it for use in training predictive models.

Activity 2: Preparing to Train a Predictive Model for the Employee-Retention Problem

Suppose you are hired to do freelance work for a company who wants to find insights into why their employees are leaving. They have compiled a set of data they think will be helpful in this respect. It includes details on employee satisfaction levels, evaluations, time spent at work, department, and salary.

The company shares their data with you by sending you a file called hr_data.csv and asking what you think can be done to help stop employees from leaving.

Our aim is to

apply the concepts you've learned thus far to a real-life problem. In particular, we seek to:

1. Determine a plan for using predictive analytics to provide impactful business insights, given the available data.

2. Prepare the data for use in machine learning models.

> **Note**
>
> Starting with this activity and continuing through the remainder of this chapter, we'll be using Human Resources Analytics dataset, which is a Kaggle dataset. The link to the dataset can be found here: https://bit.ly/2OXWFUs. The data is simulated, meaning the samples are artificially generated and do not represent real people. We'll ignore this fact as we analyze and model the data. There is a small difference between the dataset we use in this book and the online version. Our human resource analytics data contains some NaN values. These were manually removed from the online version of the dataset, for the purposes of illustrating data cleaning techniques. We have also added a column of data called is_smoker, for the same purposes.

In order to achieve this, following steps have to be executed:

1. Scroll to the **Activity A** section of the **lesson-2-workbook.ipynb** notebook file.

2. Check the head of the table to verify that it is in standard CSV format.

3. Load the data with Pandas.

4. Inspect the columns by printing **df.columns** and make sure the data has loaded as expected by printing the DataFrame **head** and **tail** with **df.head()** and **df.tail()**:

5. Check the number of rows (including the header) in the CSV file.

6. Compare this result to **len(df)** to make sure we've loaded all the data:

7. Assess the target variable and check the distribution and number of missing entries.

8. Print the data type of each feature.

9. Display the feature distributions.

10. Check how many **NaN** values are in each column by running the following code:

11. Drop the **is_smoker** column as there is barely any information in this metric.

12. Fill the **NaN** values in the **time_spend_company** column.

13. Make a boxplot of **average_montly_hours** segmented by **number_project**.

14. Calculate the mean of each group by running the following code:

15. Fill the **NaN** values in **average_montly_hours**.

16. Confirm that **df** has no more **NaN** values by running the assertion test.

17. Transform the string and Boolean fields into integer representations.

18. Print **df.columns** to show the fields

19. Save our preprocessed data.

> **Note**
>
> The detailed steps along with the solutions are presented in the *Appendix A* (pg. no. 150).

Again, we pause here to note how well the Jupyter Notebook suited our needs when performing this initial data analysis and clean-up. Imagine, for example, we left this project in its current state for a few months. Upon returning to it, we would probably not remember what exactly was going on when we left it. Referring back to this notebook though, we would be able to retrace our steps and quickly recall what we previously learned about the data. Furthermore, we could update the data source with any new data and re-run the notebook to prepare the new set of data for use in our machine learning algorithms. Recall that in this situation, it would be best to make a copy of the notebook first, so as not to lose the initial analysis.

To summarize, you've learned and applied methods for preparing to train a machine learning model. We started by discussing steps for identifying a problem that can be solved with predictive analytics. This consisted of:

- Looking at the available data

- Determining the business needs

- Assessing the data for suitability

We also discussed how to identify supervised versus unsupervised and regression versus classification problems.

After identifying our problem, we learned techniques for using Jupyter Notebooks to build and test a data transformation pipeline. These techniques included methods and best practices for filling missing data, transforming categorical features, and building train/test data sets.

In the remainder of this chapter, we will use this preprocessed data to train a variety of classification models. To avoid blindly applying algorithms we don't understand, we start by introducing them and overviewing how they work. Then, we use Jupyter to train and compare their predictive capabilities. Here, we have the opportunity to discuss more advanced topics in machine learning like overfitting, k-fold cross-validation, and validation curves.

Training Classification Models

As you've already seen in the previous chapter, using libraries such as scikit-learn and platforms such as Jupyter, predictive models can be trained in just a few lines of code. This is possible by abstracting away the difficult computations involved with optimizing model parameters. In other words, we deal with a black box where the internal operations are hidden instead. With this simplicity also comes the danger of misusing algorithms, for example, by overfitting during training or failing to properly test on unseen data. We'll show how to avoid these pitfalls while training classification models and produce trustworthy results with the use of k-fold cross validation and validation curves.

Introduction to Classification Algorithms

Recall the two types of supervised machine learning: regression and classification. In regression, we predict a continuous target variable. For example, recall the linear and polynomial models from the first chapter. In this chapter, we focus on the other type of supervised machine learning: classification. Here, the goal is to predict the class of a sample using the available metrics.

In the simplest case, there are only two possible classes, which means we are doing binary classification. This is the case for the example problem in this chapter, where we try to predict whether an employee has left or not. If we have more than two class labels instead, we are doing multi-class classification.

Although there is little difference between binary and multi-class classification when training models with scikit-learn, what's done inside the "black box" is notably different. In particular, multi-class classification models often use the one-versus-rest method. This works as follows for a case with three class labels. When the model is "fit" with the data, three models are trained, and each model predicts whether the sample is part of an individual class or part of some other class. This might bring to mind the one-hot encoding for features that we did earlier. When a prediction is made for a sample, the class label with the highest confidence level is returned.

In this chapter, we'll train three types of classification models: Support Vector Machines, Random Forests, and k-Nearest Neighbors classifiers. Each of these algorithms are quite different. As we will see, however, they are quite similar to train and use for predictions thanks to scikit-learn. Before swapping over to the Jupyter Notebook and implementing these, we'll briefly see how they work.

SVMs attempt to find the best hyperplane to divide classes by. This is done by maximizing the distance between the hyperplane and the closest samples of each class, which are called support vectors.

This linear method can also be used to model nonlinear classes using the kernel trick. This method maps the features into a higher-dimensional space in which the hyperplane is determined. This hyperplane is also referred to as the decision surface, and we'll visualize it when training our models.

K-Nearest Neighbors classification algorithms memorize the training data and make predictions depending on the K nearest samples in the feature space. With three features, this can be visualized as a sphere surrounding the prediction sample. Often, however, we are dealing with more than three features and therefore hyperspheres are drawn to find the closest K samples.

Random Forests are an ensemble of decision trees, where each has been trained on different subsets of the training data.

A decision tree algorithm classifies a sample based on a series of decisions. For example, the first decision might be "if feature x_1 is less than or greater than 0." The data would then be split on this condition and fed into descending branches of the tree. Each step in the decision tree is decided based on the feature split that maximizes the information gain. Essentially, this term describes the mathematics that attempts to pick the best possible split of the target variable.

Training a Random Forest consists of creating bootstrapped (that is, randomly sampled data with replacement) datasets for a set of decision trees. Predictions are then made based on the majority vote. These have the benefit of less overfitting and better generalizability.

> **Note**
>
> Decision trees can be used to model a mix of continuous and categorical data, which make them very useful. Furthermore, as we will see later in this chapter, the tree depth can be limited to reduce overfitting. For a detailed (but brief) look into the decision tree algorithm, check out this popular StackOverflow answer: https://stackoverflow.com/a/1859910/3511819. There, the author shows a simple example and discusses concepts such as node purity, information gain, and entropy.

Exercise 9: Training Two-Feature Classification Models With Scikit-learn

We'll continue working on the employee retention problem that we introduced in the first topic. We previously prepared a dataset for training a classification model, in which we predicted whether an employee has left or not. Now, we'll take that data and use it to train classification models:

1. Start the **NotebookApp** and open the **lesson-2-workbook.ipynb** file. Scroll down to **Topic B: Training classification models**. Run the first couple of cells to set the default figure size and load the processed data that we previously saved to a CSV file. For this example, we'll be training classification models on two continuous features: **satisfaction_level and last_evaluation**.

2. Draw the bivariate and univariate graphs of the continuous target variables by running the cell with the following code:

```
sns.jointplot('satisfaction_level', 'last_evaluation', data=df,
kind='hex')
```

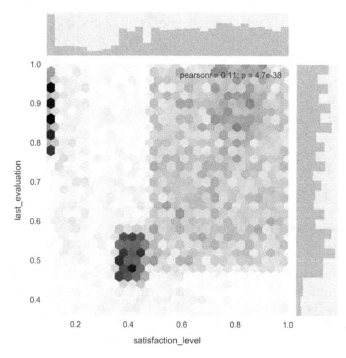

Figure 2.23: Bivariate and univariate graphs for satisfaction_level and last_evaluation

As you can see in the preceding image, there are some very distinct patterns in the data.

3. Re-plot the bivariate distribution, segmenting on the target variable, by running the cell containing the following code:

```
plot_args = dict(shade=True, shade_lowest=False) for i, c in zip((0, 1),
('Reds', 'Blues')):
sns.kdeplot(df.loc[df.left==i, 'satisfaction_level'], df.loc[df.left==i,
'last_evaluation'], cmap=c, **plot_args)
```

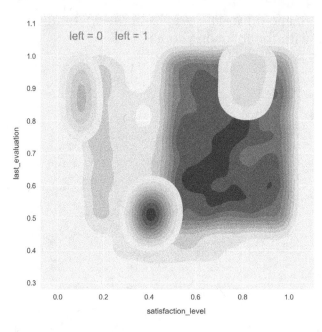

Figure 2.24: Bivariate distribution for satisfaction_level and last_evaluation

Now, we can see how the patterns are related to the target variable. For the remainder of this exercise, we'll try to exploit these patterns to train effective classification models.

4. Split the data into training and test sets by running the cell containing the following code:

```
from sklearn.model_selection import train_test_split
features = ['satisfaction_level', 'last_evaluation'] X_train, X_test, y_
train, y_test = train_test_split(
df[features].values, df['left'].values, test_size=0.3, random_state=1)
```

Our first two models, the Support Vector Machine and k-Nearest Neighbors algorithm, are most effective when the input data is scaled so that all of the features are on the same order. We'll accomplish this with scikit-learn's **StandardScaler**.

5. Load **StandardScaler** and create a new instance, as referenced by the scaler variable. Fit the scaler on the training set and transform it. Then, transform the test set. Run the cell containing the following code:

```
from sklearn.preprocessing import StandardScaler scaler = StandardScaler()
X_train_std = scaler.fit_transform(X_train) X_test_std = scaler.
transform(X_test)
```

> **Note**
>
> An easy mistake to make when doing machine learning is to "fit" the scaler on the whole dataset, when in fact it should only be "fit" to the training data. For example, scaling the data before splitting into training and testing sets is a mistake. We don't want this because the model training should not be influenced in any way by the test data.

6. Import the scikit-learn support vector machine class and fit the model on the training data by running the cell containing the following code:

```
from sklearn.svm import SVC
svm = SVC(kernel='linear', C=1, random_state=1) svm.fit(X_train_std, y_
train)
```

7. Compute the accuracy of this model on unseen data by running the cell containing the following code:

```
from sklearn.metrics import accuracy_score y_pred = svm.predict(X_test_
std)
acc = accuracy_score(y_test, y_pred) print('accuracy = {:.1f}%'.
format(acc*100))
>> accuracy = 75.9%
```

8. We predict the targets for our test samples and then use scikit-learn's **accuracy_score** function to determine the accuracy. The result looks promising at ~75%! Not bad for our first model. Recall, though, the target is imbalanced. Let's see how accurate the predictions are for each class.

9. Calculate the confusion matrix and then determine the accuracy within each class by running the cell containing the following code:

```
from sklearn.metrics import confusion_matrix cmat = confusion_matrix(y_
test, y_pred)
scores = cmat.diagonal() / cmat.sum(axis=1) * 100 print('left = 0 :
{:.2f}%'.format(scores[0]))
print('left = 1 : {:.2f}%'.format(scores[1]))
>> left = 0 : 100.00%
>> left = 1 : 0.00%
```

It looks like the model is simply classifying every sample as 0, which is clearly not helpful at all. Let's use a contour plot to show the predicted class at each point in the feature space. This is commonly known as the decision- regions plot.

10. Plot the decision regions using a helpful function from the **mlxtend** library. Run the cell containing the following code:

```
from mlxtend.plotting import plot_decision_regions N_samples = 200
X, y = X_train_std[:N_samples], y_train[:N_samples] plot_decision_
regions(X, y, clf=svm)
```

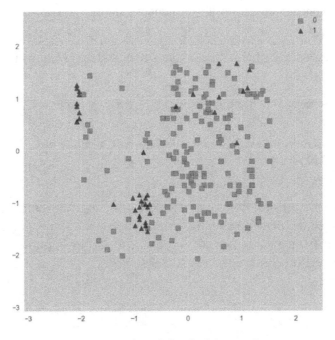

Figure 2.25: Plot of the decision regions

The function plots decision regions along with a set of samples passed as arguments. In order to see the decision regions properly without too many samples obstructing our view, we pass only a 200-sample subset of the test data to the `plot_decision_regions` function. In this case, of course, it does not matter. We see the result is entirely red, indicating every point in the feature space would be classified as 0.

It shouldn't be surprising that a linear model can't do a good job of describing these nonlinear patterns. Recall earlier we mentioned the kernel trick for using SVMs to classify nonlinear problems. Let's see if doing this can improve the result.

11. Print the docstring for scikit-learn's SVM by running the cell containing SVC. Scroll down and check out the parameter descriptions. Notice the kernel option, which is actually enabled by default as **rbf**. Use this **kernel** option to train a new SVM by running the cell containing the following code:

```
check_model_fit(svm, X_test_std, y_test)
```

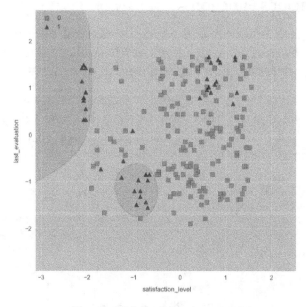

Figure 2.26: Training a new SVM

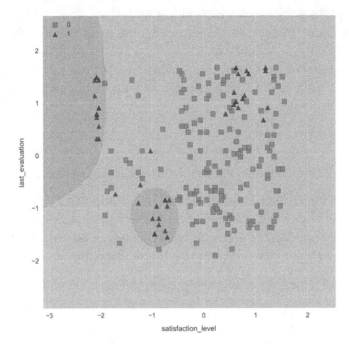

Figure 2.27: Enhanced results with non-linear patterns

The result is much better. Now, we are able to capture some of the non-linear patterns in the data and correctly classify the majority of the employees who have left.

The plot_decision_regions Function

The **plot_decision_regions** function is provided by **mlxtend**, a Python library developed by Sebastian Raschka. It's worth taking a peek at the source code (which is of course written in Python) to understand how these plots are drawn. It's really not too complicated.

In a Jupyter Notebook, import the function with **from mlxtend.plotting import plot_decision_regions** and then pull up the help with **plot_decision_regions?** and scroll to the bottom to see the local file path:

```
In [152]:  from mlxtend.plotting import plot_decision_regions
           plot_decision_regions?

Returns
---------
ax : matplotlib.axes.Axes object
File:       ~/anaconda/lib/python3.5/site-packages/mlxtend/plotting/decision_regions.py
Type:       function
```

Figure 2.28: Local file path

Then, open up the file and read through it. For example, you could run **cat** in the notebook:

```
In [153]:  cat ~/anaconda/lib/python3.5/site-packages/mlxtend/plotting/decision_regions.py

           def plot_decision_regions(X, y, clf,
                                     feature_index=None,
                                     filler_feature_values=None,
                                     filler_feature_ranges=None,
                                     ax=None,
                                     X_highlight=None,
                                     res=0.02, legend=1,
                                     hide_spines=True,
                                     markers='s^oxv<>',
                                     colors='red,blue,limegreen,gray,cyan'):
               """Plot decision regions of a classifier.

               Please note that this functions assumes that class labels are
               labeled consecutively, e.g,. 0, 1, 2, 3, 4, and 5. If you have class
               labels with integer labels > 4, you may want to provide additional colors
               and/or markers as `colors` and `markers` arguments.
               See http://matplotlib.org/examples/color/named_colors.html for more
               information.
```

Figure 2.29: Running cat in the notebook

This is okay, but not ideal as there's no color markup for the code. It's better to copy it (so you don't accidentally alter the original) and open it with your favorite text editor.

When drawing attention to the code responsible for mapping the decision regions, we see a contour plot of predictions Z over an array **X_predict** that spans the feature space.

```
xx, yy = np.meshgrid(np.arange(x_min, x_max, xres),
                     np.arange(y_min, y_max, yres))

if dim == 1:
    X_predict = np.array([xx.ravel()]).T
else:
    X_grid = np.array([xx.ravel(), yy.ravel()]).T
    X_predict = np.zeros((X_grid.shape[0], dim))
    X_predict[:, x_index] = X_grid[:, 0]
    X_predict[:, y_index] = X_grid[:, 1]
    if dim > 2:
        for feature_idx in filler_feature_values:
            X_predict[:, feature_idx] = filler_feature_values[feature_idx]
Z = clf.predict(X_predict)
Z = Z.reshape(xx.shape)
# Plot decisoin region
ax.contourf(xx, yy, Z,
            alpha=0.3,
            colors=colors,
            levels=np.arange(Z.max() + 2) - 0.5)
```

Figure 2.30: The screenshot of the code for mapping decision regions

Let's move to training our model on k-Nearest Neighbors.

Exercise 10: Training K-nearest Neighbors for Our Model

1. Load the scikit-learn KNN classification model and print the docstring by running the cell containing the following code:

    ```
    from sklearn.neighbors import KNeighborsClassifier KNeighborsClassifier?
    ```

    The **n_neighbors** parameter decides how many samples to use when making a classification. If the weights parameter is set to uniform, then class labels are decided by majority vote. Another useful choice for the weights is distance, where closer samples have a higher weight in the voting. Like most model parameters, the best choice for this depends on the particular dataset.

2. Train the KNN classifier with **n_neighbors=3**, and then compute the accuracy and decision regions. Run the cell containing the following code:

    ```
    knn = KNeighborsClassifier(n_neighbors=3)
    knn.fit(X_train_std, y_train)
    check_model_fit(knn, X_test_std, y_test)
    ```

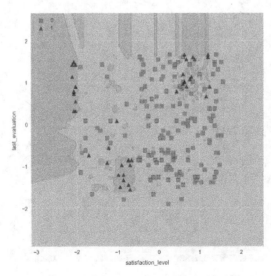

Figure 2.31: Training the kNN classifier with n_negihbours=3

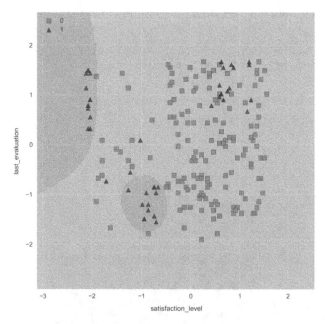

Figure 2.32: Enhanced results after training

We see an increase in overall accuracy and a significant improvement for class 1 in particular. However, the decision region plot would indicate we are overfitting the data. This is evident by the hard, "choppy" decision boundary, and small pockets of blue everywhere. We can soften the decision boundary and decrease overfitting by increasing the number of nearest neighbors.

3. Train a KNN model with **n_neighbors=25** by running the cell containing the following code:

```
knn = KNeighborsClassifier(n_neighbors=25) knn.fit(X_train_std, y_train)
check_model_fit(knn, X_test_std, y_test)
```

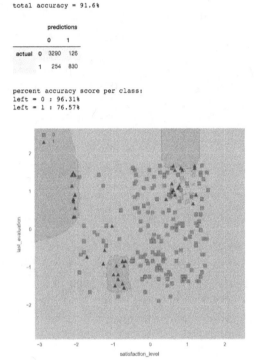

Figure 2.33: Training the kNN classifier with n_negihbours=25

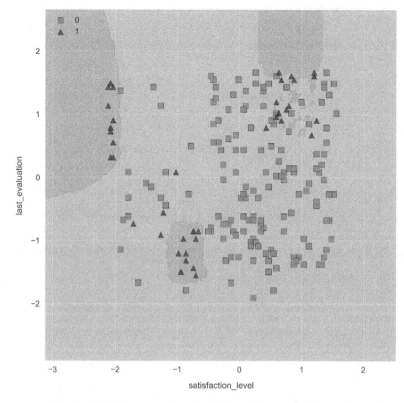

Figure 2.34: Output after training with n_neighbours=25

As we can see, the decision boundaries are significantly less choppy, and there are far less pockets of blue. The accuracy for class 1 is slightly less, but we would need to use a more comprehensive method such as k-fold cross validation to decide if there's a significant difference between the two models.

Note that increasing **n_neighbors** has no effect on training time, as the model is simply memorizing the data. The prediction time, however, will be greatly affected.

> **Note**
>
> When doing machine learning with real-world data, it's important for the algorithms to run quick enough to serve their purposes. For example, a script to predict tomorrow's weather that takes longer than a day to run is completely useless! Memory is also a consideration that should be taken into account when dealing with substantial amounts of data.

We will now train a Random Forest.

Exercise 11: Training a Random Forest

> **Note**
>
> Observe how similar it is to train and make predictions on each model, despite them each being so different internally.

1. Train a Random Forest classification model composed of 50 decision trees, each with a max depth of 5. Run the cell containing the following code:

```
from sklearn.ensemble import RandomForestClassifier
forest = RandomForestClassifier(n_estimators=50, max_depth=5,
random_state=1)
forest.fit(X_train, y_train) check_model_fit(forest, X_test, y_test)
```

```
total accuracy = 92.0%

              predictions
              0     1

    actual 0  3371   45

           1   317  767


percent accuracy score per class:
left = 0 : 98.68%
left = 1 : 70.76%
```

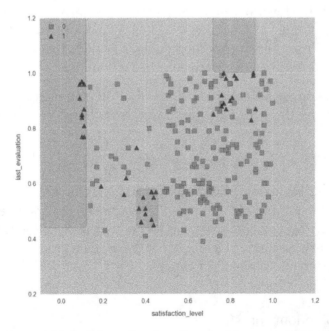

Figure 2.35: Training a Random Forest with a max depth of 5

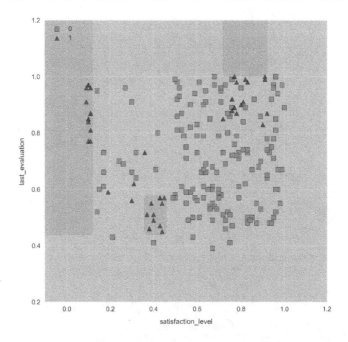

Figure 2.36: Output after training with a max depth of 5

Note the distinctive axes-parallel decision boundaries produced by decision tree machine learning algorithms.

We can access any of the individual decision trees used to build the Random Forest. These trees are stored in the **estimators_attribute** of the model. Let's draw one of these decision trees to get a feel for what's going on. Doing this requires the **graphviz** dependency, which can sometimes be difficult to install.

2. Draw one of the decision trees in the Jupyter Notebook by running the cell containing the following code:

```
from sklearn.tree import export_graphviz import graphviz
dot_data = export_graphviz(
forest.estimators_[0], out_file=None, feature_names=features, class_
names=['no', 'yes'], filled=True, rounded=True, special_characters=True)
graph = graphviz.Source(dot_data) graph
```

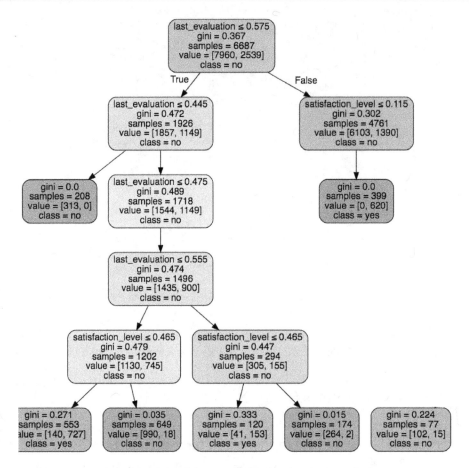

Figure 2.37: Decision tree obtained using graphviz

We can see that each path is limited to five nodes as a result of setting max_depth=5. The orange boxes represent predictions of no (has not left the company), and the blue boxes represent yes (has left the company). The shade of each box (light, dark, and so on) indicates the confidence level, which is related to the gini value.

To summarize, we have accomplished two of the learning objectives in this section:

- We gained a qualitative understanding of support vector machines (SVMs), k-Nearest Neighbor classifiers (kNNs), and Random Forest

- We are now able to train a variety of models using scikit-learn and Jupyter Notebooks so that we can confidently build and compare predictive models

In particular, we used the preprocessed data from our employee retention problem to train classification models to predict whether an employee has left the company or not. For the purposes of keeping things simple and focusing on the algorithms, we built models to predict this given only two features: the satisfaction level and last evaluation value. This two-dimensional feature space also allowed us to visualize the decision boundaries and identify what overfitting looks like.

In the following section, we will introduce two important topics in machine learning: k-fold cross-validation and validation curves.

Assessing Models With K-fold Cross-Validation and Validation Curves

Thus far, we have trained models on a subset of the data and then assessed performance on the unseen portion, called the test set. This is good practice because the model performance on training data is not a good indicator of its effectiveness as a predictor. It's very easy to increase accuracy on a training dataset by overfitting a model, which can result in poorer performance on unseen data.

That said, simply training models on data split in this way is not good enough. There is a natural variance in data that causes accuracies to be different (if even slightly) depending on the training and test splits. Furthermore, using only one training/ test split to compare models can introduce bias towards certain models and lead to overfitting.

K-fold cross validation offers a solution to this problem and allows the variance to be accounted for by way of an error estimate on each accuracy calculation. This, in turn, naturally leads to the use of validation curves for tuning model parameters. These plot the accuracy as a function of a hyper parameter such as the number of decision trees used in a Random Forest or the max depth.

> **Note**
>
> This is our first time using the term hyperparameter. It references a parameter that is defined when initializing a model, for example, the C parameter of the SVM. This is in contradistinction to a parameter of the trained model, such as the equation of the decision boundary hyperplane for a trained SVM.

The method is illustrated in the following diagram, where we see how the k-folds can be selected from the dataset:

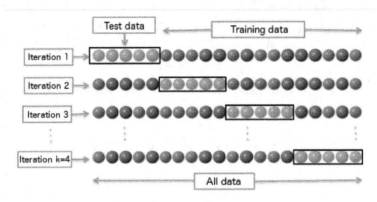

Figure 2.38: Selecting k-folds from a data set

The k-fold cross validation algorithm goes as follows:

1. Split data into k "folds" of near-equal size.

2. Test and train k models on different fold combinations. Each model will include k - 1 folds of training data and the left-out fold is used for testing. In this method, each fold ends up being used as the validation data exactly once.

3. Calculate the model accuracy by taking the mean of the k values. The standard deviation is also calculated to provide error bars on the value.

It's standard to set $k = 10$, but smaller values for k should be considered if using a big data set.

This validation method can be used to reliably compare model performance with different hyperparameters (for example, the C parameter for an SVM or the number of nearest neighbors in a KNN classifier). It's also suitable for comparing entirely different models.

Once the *best model* has been identified, it should be re-trained on the entirety of the dataset before being used to predict actual classifications.

When implementing this with scikit-learn, it's common to use a slightly improved variation of the normal k-fold algorithm instead. This is called **stratified k-fold**. The improvement is that stratified k-fold cross validation maintains roughly even class label populations in the folds. As you can imagine, this reduces the overall variance in the models and decreases the likelihood of highly unbalanced models causing bias.

Validation curves are plots of a training and validation metric as a function of some model parameter. They allow to us to make good model parameter selections. In this book, we will use the accuracy score as our metric for these plots.

> **Note**
>
> The documentation for plot validation curves is available here: http://scikit-learn. org/stable/auto_examples/ model_selection/plot_validation_curve.html.

Consider this validation curve, where the accuracy score is plotted as a function of the gamma SVM parameter:

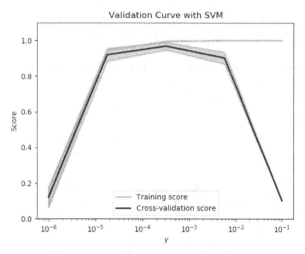

Figure 2.39: Validation curve with SVM

Starting on the left side of the plot, we can see that both sets of data are agreeing on the score, which is good. However, the score is also quite low compared to other gamma values, so therefore we say the model is underfitting the data. Increasing the gamma, we can see a point where the error bars of these two lines no longer overlap. From this point on, we see the classifier overfitting the data as the models behave increasingly well on the training set compared to the validation set. The optimal value for the gamma parameter can be found by looking for a high validation score with overlapping error bars on the two lines.

Keep in mind that a learning curve for some parameter is only valid while the other parameters remain constant. For example, if training the SVM in this plot, we could decide to pick gamma on the order of. However, we may want to optimize the **C** parameter as well. With a different value for **C**, the preceding plot would be different and our selection for gamma may no longer be optimal.

Exercise 12: Using K-fold Cross Validation and Validation Curves in Python With Scikit-learn

1. Start the **NotebookApp** and open the **lesson-2-workbook.ipynb** file. Scroll down to **Subtopic B: K-fold cross-validation and validation curves**.

    The training data should already be in the notebook's memory, but let's reload it as a reminder of what exactly we're working with.

2. Load the data and select the **satisfaction_level** and **last_evaluation** features for the training/validation set. We will not use the train-test split this time because we are going to use k-fold validation instead. Run the cell containing the following code:

    ```
    df = pd.read_csv('../data/hr-analytics/hr_data_processed. csv')
    features = ['satisfaction_level', 'last_evaluation']
    X = df[features].values y = df.left.values
    ```

3. Instantiate a Random Forest model by running the cell containing the following code:

    ```
    clf = RandomForestClassifier(n_estimators=100, max_depth=5)
    ```

4. To train the model with stratified k-fold cross validation, we'll use the **model_selection.cross_val_score** function.

    Train 10 variations of our model **clf** using stratified k-fold validation. Note that scikit-learn's **cross_val_score** does this type of validation by default. Run the cell containing the following code:

    ```
    from sklearn.model_selection import cross_val_score np.random.seed(1)
    scores = cross_val_score(
    estimator=clf, X=X,
    y=y, cv=10)
    print('accuracy = {:.3f} +/- {:.3f}'.format(scores.mean(), scores.std()))
    >> accuracy = 0.923 +/- 0.005
    ```

    Note how we use **np.random.seed** to set the seed for the random number generator, therefore ensuring reproducibility with respect to the randomly selected samples for each fold and decision tree in the Random Forest.

5. Calculate the accuracy as the average of each fold. We can also see the individual accuracies for each fold by printing scores. To see these, **run print(scores)**:

    ```
    >> array([ 0.93404397,   0.91533333,   0.92266667,
    0.91866667, 0.92133333,
    0.92866667, 0.91933333,  0.92   ,
    ```

```
0.92795197, 0.92128085])
```

Using **cross_val_score** is very convenient, but it doesn't tell us about the accuracies within each class. We can do this manually with the **model_ selection. StratifiedKFold** class. This class takes the number of folds as an initialization parameter, then the split method is used to build randomly sampled "masks" for the data. A mask is simply an array containing indexes of items in another array, where the items can then be returned by doing this: **data[mask]**.

6. Define a custom class for calculating k-fold cross validation class accuracies. Run the cell containing the following code:

```
from sklearn.model_selection import StratifiedKFold

...

...

print('fold: {:d} accuracy: {:s}'.format(k+1, str(class_acc)))
return class_accuracy
```

> **Note**
>
> For the complete code, refer to the following: https://bit.ly/2O5uP3h.

7. We can then calculate the class accuracies with code that's very similar to step 4. Do this by running the cell containing the following code:

```
from sklearn.model_selection import cross_val_score np.random.seed(1)

...

...

>> fold: 10 accuracy: [ 0.98861646    0.70588235]
>> accuracy = [ 0.98722476     0.71715647] +/- [ 0.00330026
0.02326823]
```

> **Note**
>
> For the complete code, refer to the following: https://bit.ly/2EKK7Lp.

8. Now we can see the class accuracies for each fold! Pretty neat, right?

9. Calculate a validation curve using **model_selection.validation_curve**. This function uses stratified k-fold cross validation to train models for various values of a given parameter.

Do the calculations required to plot a validation curve by training Random Forests over a range of **max_depth** values. Run the cell containing the following code:

```
from sklearn.model_selection import validation_curve
clf = RandomForestClassifier(n_estimators=10) max_depths = np.arange(3, 16, 3)
train_scores, test_scores = validation_curve( estimator=clf,
X=X,
y=y, param_name='max_depth', param_range=max_depths,
cv=10);
```

This will return arrays with the cross validation scores for each model, where the models have different max depths. In order to visualize the results, we'll leverage a function provided in the scikit-learn documentation.

10. Run the cell in which **plot_validation_curve** is defined. Then, run the cell containing the following code to draw the plot:

```
plot_validation_curve(train_scores, test_scores,
max_depths, xlabel='max_depth')
```

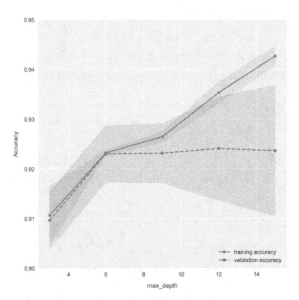

Figure 2.40: Plot validation curve

Recall how setting the max depth for decision trees limits the amount of overfitting. This is reflected in the validation curve, where we see overfitting taking place for large max depth values to the right. A good value for **max_depth** appears to be 6, where we see the training and validation accuracies in agreement. When **max_depth** is equal to 3, we see the model underfitting the data as training and validation accuracies are lower.

To summarize, we have learned and implemented two important techniques for building reliable predictive models. The first such technique was k-foldcross-validation, which is used to split the data into various train/test batches and generate a set accuracy. From this set, we then calculated the average accuracy and the standard deviation as a measure of the error. This is important so that we have a gauge of the variability of our model and we can produce trustworthy accuracy.

We also learned about another such technique to ensure we have trustworthy results: validation curves. These allow us to visualize when our model is overfitting based on comparing training and validation accuracies. By plotting the curve over a range of our selected hyperparameter, we are able to identify its optimal value.

In the final section of this chapter, we take everything we have learned so far and put it together in order to build our final predictive model for the employee retention problem. We seek to improve the accuracy, compared to the models trained thus far, by including all of the features from the dataset in our model. We'll see now-familiar topics such as k-fold cross-validation and validation curves, but we'll also introduce something new: dimensionality reduction techniques.

Dimensionality Reduction Techniques

Dimensionality reduction can simply involve removing unimportant features from the training data, but more exotic methods exist, such as **Principal Component Analysis** (**PCA**) and Linear Discriminant Analysis (LDA). These techniques allow for data compression, where the most important information from a large group of features can be encoded in just a few features.

In this subtopic, we'll focus on PCA. This technique transforms the data by projecting it into a new subspace of orthogonal "principal components," where the components with the highest eigenvalues encode the most information for training the model. Then, we can simply select a few of these principal components in place of the original high-dimensional dataset. For example, PCA could be used to encode the information from every pixel in an image. In this case, the original feature space would have dimensions equal to the number of pixels in the image. This high-dimensional space could then be reduced with PCA, where the majority of useful information for training predictive models might be reduced to just a few dimensions. Not only does this save time when training and using models, it allows them to perform better by removing noise in the dataset.

Like the models you've seen, it's not necessary to have a detailed understanding of PCA in order to leverage the benefits. However, we'll dig into the technical details of PCA just a bit further so that we can conceptualize it better. The key insight of PCA is to identify patterns between features based on correlations, so the PCA algorithm calculates the covariance matrix and then decomposes this into eigenvectors and eigenvalues. The vectors are then used to transform the data into a new subspace, from which a fixed number of principal components can be selected.

In the following exercise, we'll see an example of how PCA can be used to improve our Random Forest model for the employee retention problem we have been working on. This will be done after training a classification model on the full feature space, to see how our accuracy is affected by dimensionality reduction.

Exercise 13: Training a Predictive Model for the Employee Retention Problem

We have already spent considerable effort planning a machine learning strategy, preprocessing the data, and building predictive models for the employee retention problem. Recall that our business objective was to help the client prevent employees from leaving. The strategy we decided upon was to build a classification model that would predict the probability of employees leaving. This way, the company can assess the likelihood of current employees leaving and take action to prevent it.

Given our strategy, we can summarize the type of predictive modeling we are doing as follows:

- Supervised learning on labeled training data
- Classification problems with two class labels (binary)

In particular, we are training models to determine whether an employee has left the company, given a set of continuous and categorical features. After preparing the data for machine learning in *Activity 1, Preparing to Train a Predictive Model for the Employee-Retention Problem*, we went on to implement SVM, k-Nearest Neighbors, and Random Forest algorithms using just two features. These models were able to make predictions with over 90% overall accuracy. When looking at the specific class accuracies, however, we found that employees who had left (`class- label 1`) could only be predicted with 70-80% accuracy.

Let's see how much this can be improved by utilizing the full feature space.

1. Scroll down to the code for this section in the `lesson-2-workbook.ipynb` notebook. We should already have the preprocessed data loaded from the previous exercises, but this can be done again, if desired, by executing `df = pd.read_csv('../data/ hr-analytics/hr_data_processed.csv')`. Then, print the DataFrame columns with `print(df.columns)`.

2. Define a list of all the features by copy and pasting the output from **df.columns** into a new list (making sure to remove the target variable **left**). Then, define **X** and **Y** as we have done before. This goes as follows:

```
features = ['satisfaction_level', 'last_evaluation', 'number_project',
'average_montly_hours', 'time_spend_company', 'work_ accident',
...
...
X = df[features].values y = df.left.values
```

> **Note**
>
> For the complete code, refer to the following: https://bit.ly/2D3WOQ2.

Looking at the feature names, recall what the values look like for each one. Scroll up to the set of histograms we made in the first activity to help jog your memory. The first two features are continuous; these are what we used for training models in the previous two exercises. After that, we have a few discrete features, such as **number_project** and **time_spend_company**, followed by some binary fields such as **work_accident** and **promotion_last_5years**. We also have a bunch of binary features, such as **department_ IT** and **department_accounting**, which were created by one-hot encoding.

Given a mix of features like this, Random Forests are a very attractive type of model. For one thing, they're compatible with feature sets composed of both continuous and categorical data, but this is not particularly special; for instance, an SVM can be trained on mixed feature types as well (given proper preprocessing).

> **Note**
>
> If you're interested in training an SVM or k-Nearest Neighbors classifier on mixed-type input features, you can use the data-scaling prescription from this StackExchange answer: https://stats.stackexchange.com/questions/82923/mixing-continuous-and-binary-data-with-linear-svm/83086#83086.

A simple approach would be to preprocess data as follows:

standardize continuous variables; one-hot-encode categorical features; shift binary values to -1 and 1 instead of 0 and 1. Finally, the mixed-feature data could be used to train a variety of classification models.

3. Tune the **max_depth** hyperparameter using a validation curve to figure out the best parameters for our Random Forest model. Calculate the training and validation accuracies by running the following code:

```
%%time np.random.seed(1)
clf = RandomForestClassifier(n_estimators=20) max_depths = [3, 4, 5, 6, 7,
9, 12, 15, 18, 21]
train_scores, test_scores = validation_curve( estimator=clf,
X=X,
y=y, param_name='max_depth', param_range=max_depths,
cv=5);
```

We are testing 10 models with k-fold cross validation. By setting k = 5, we produce five estimates of the accuracy for each model, from which we extract the mean and standard deviation to plot in the validation curve. In total, we train 50 models, and since **n_estimators** is set to 20, we are training a total of 1,000 decision trees! All in roughly 10 seconds!

4. Plot the validation curve using our custom **plot_validation_curve** function from the last exercise. Run the following code:

```
plot_validation_curve(train_scores, test_scores,
max_depths, xlabel='max_depth');
```

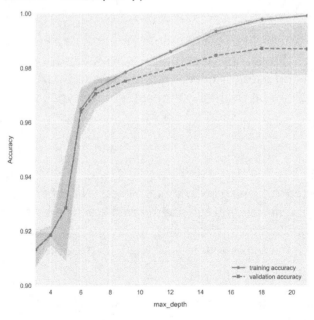

Figure 2.41: Plot validation curve for different values of max_depths

For small max depths, we see the model underfitting the data. Total accuracies dramatically increase by allowing the decision trees to be deeper and encode more complicated patterns in the data. As the max depth is increased further and the accuracy approaches 100%, we find the model overfits the data, causing the training and validation accuracies to grow apart. Based on this figure, let's select a max_depth of 6 for our model.

We should really do the same for n_estimators, but in the spirit of saving time, we'll skip it. You are welcome to plot it on your own; you should find agreement between training and validation sets for a large range of values. Usually it's better to use more decision tree estimators in the random forest, but this comes at the cost of increased training times. We'll use 200 estimators to train our model.

5. Use cross_val_class_score, the k-fold cross validation by class function we created earlier, to test the selected model, a Random Forest with max_ depth = 6 and n_estimators = 200:

```
np.random.seed(1)
clf = RandomForestClassifier(n_estimators=200, max_depth=6) scores = cross_
val_class_score(clf, X, y)
print('accuracy = {} +/- {}'\
.format(scores.mean(axis=0), scores.std(axis=0)))
>> accuracy = [ 0.99553722      0.85577359] +/- [ 0.00172575
0.02614334]
```

The accuracies are way higher now that we're using the full feature set, compared to before when we only had the two continuous features!

6. Visualize the accuracies with a boxplot by running the following code:

```
fig = plt.figure(figsize=(5, 7)) sns.boxplot(data=pd.DataFrame(scores,
columns=[0, 1]),
palette=sns.color_palette('Set1')) plt.xlabel('Left')
plt.ylabel('Accuracy')
```

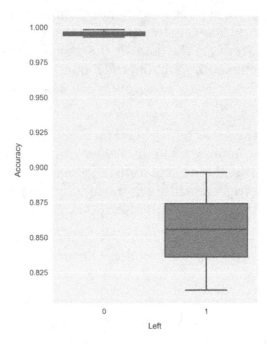

Figure 2.42: Visualizing the accuracy with a box plot

Random forests can provide an estimate of the feature performances.

> **Note**
>
> The feature importance in scikit-learn is calculated based on how the node impurity changes with respect to each feature. For a more detailed explanation, take a look at the following StackOverflow thread about how feature importance is determined in Random Forest Classifier: https://stackoverflow.com

7. Plot the feature importance, as stored in the attribute **feature_importances_**, by running the following code:

```
pd.Series(clf.feature_importances_, name='Feature importance',
index=df[features].columns)\
.sort_values()\
.plot.barh() plt.xlabel('Feature importance')
```

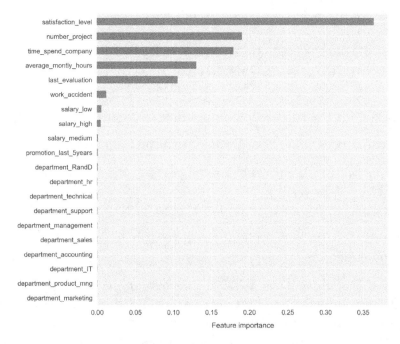

Figure 2.43: Plot of feature_importance

8. It doesn't look like we're getting much in the way of useful contribution from the one-hot encoded variables: department and salary. Also, the **promotion_last_5years** and **work_accident** features don't appear to be very useful.

    Let's use PCA to condense all of these weak features into just a few principal components.

9. Import the **PCA** class from scikit-learn and transform the features. Run the following code

    ```
    from sklearn.decomposition import PCA pca_features = \
    ...

    ...
    pca = PCA(n_components=3)
    X_pca = pca.fit_transform(X_reduce)
    ```

    > **Note**
    >
    > For the complete code, refer to the following: https://bit.ly/2D3iKL2. View the string representation of **X_pca** by typing it alone and executing the cell:

    ```
    >> array([[-0.67733089,  0.75837169, -0.10493685],
    >>    [ 0.73616575,0.77155888, -0.11046422],
    ```

```
>>      [ 0.73616575,0.77155888, -0.11046422],
>>      ...,
>>      [-0.67157059, -0.3337546 ,0.70975452],
>>      [-0.67157059, -0.3337546 ,0.70975452],
>>      [-0.67157059, -0.3337546 ,0.70975452]])
```

Since we asked for the top three components, we get three vectors returned.

10. Add the new features to our DataFrame with the following code:

```
df['first_principle_component'] = X_pca.T[0] df['second_principle_
component'] = X_pca.T[1]
df['third_principle_component'] = X_pca.T[2]
```

Select our reduced-dimension feature set to train a new Random Forest with. Run the following code:

```
features = ['satisfaction_level', 'number_project', 'time_spend_company',
'average_montly_hours', 'last_evaluation', 'first_principle_component',
'second_principle_component', 'third_principle_component']
X = df[features].values y = df.left.values
```

11. Assess the new model's accuracy with k-fold cross validation. This can be done by running the same code as before, where X now points to different features. The code is as follows:

```
np.random.seed(1)
clf = RandomForestClassifier(n_estimators=200, max_depth=6) scores = cross_
val_class_score(clf, X, y)
print('accuracy = {} +/- {}'\
.format(scores.mean(axis=0), scores.std(axis=0)))
>> accuracy = [ 0.99562463      0.90618594] +/- [ 0.00166047
0.01363927]
```

12. Visualize the result in the same way as before, using a box plot. The code is as follows:

```
fig = plt.figure(figsize=(5, 7)) sns.boxplot(data=pd.DataFrame(scores,
columns=[0, 1]), palette=sns.color_palette('Set1')) plt.xlabel('Left')
plt.ylabel('Accuracy')
```

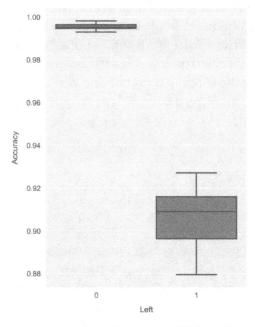

Figure 2.44: Box plot to visualize accuracy

Comparing this to the previous result, we find an improvement in the class 1 accuracy! Now, the majority of the validation sets return an accuracy greater than 90%. The average accuracy of 90.6% can be compared to the accuracy of 85.6% prior to dimensionality reduction!

Let's select this as our final model. We'll need to re-train it on the full sample space before using it in production.

13. Train the final predictive model by running the following code:

```
np.random.seed(1)
clf = RandomForestClassifier(n_estimators=200, max_depth=6) clf.fit(X, y)
```

14. Save the trained model to a binary file using **externals.joblib.dump**. Run the following code:

```
from sklearn.externals import joblib joblib.dump(clf, 'random-forest-trained.pkl')
```

15. Check that it's saved into the working directory, for example, by running:

!ls *.pkl. Then, test that we can load the model from the file by running the following code:

```
clf = joblib.load('random-forest-trained.pkl')
```

Congratulations! You've trained the final predictive model! Now, let's see an example of how it can be used to provide business insights for the client. Say we have a particular employee, who we'll call Sandra. Management has noticed she is working very hard and reported low job satisfaction in a recent survey. They would therefore like to know how likely it is that she will quit. For the sake of simplicity, let's take her feature values as a sample from the training set (but pretend that this is unseen data instead).

16. List the feature values for Sandra by running the following code:

```
sandra = df.iloc[573]
X = sandra[features]
X
>> satisfaction_level              0.360000
>> number_project                  2.000000
>> time_spend_company              3.000000
>> average_montly_hours          148.000000
>> last_evaluation                 0.470000
>> first_principle_component       0.742801
>> second_principle_component     -0.514568
>> third_principle_component      -0.677421
```

The next step is to ask the model which group it thinks she should be in.

17. Predict the class label for Sandra by running the following code:

```
clf.predict([X])
>> array([1])
```

The model classifies her as having already left the company; not a good sign! We can take this a step further and calculate the probabilities of each class label.

18. Use **clf.predict_proba** to predict the probability of our model predicting that Sandra has quit. Run the following code:

```
clf.predict_proba([X])
>> array([[ 0.06576239,   0.93423761]])
```

We see the model predicting that she has quit with 93% accuracy. Since this is clearly a red flag for management, they decide on a plan to reduce her number of monthly hours to 100 and the time spent at the company to 1.

19. Calculate the new probabilities with Sandra's newly planned metrics. Run the following code:

```
X.average_montly_hours = 100
X.time_spend_company = 1. clf.predict_proba([X])
```

```
>> array([[ 0.61070329,   0.38929671]])
```

Excellent! We can now see that the model returns a mere 38% likelihood that she has quit! Instead, it now predicts she will not have left the company.

Our model has allowed management to make a data-driven decision. By reducing her amount of time with the company by this particular amount, the model tells us that she will most likely remain an employee at the company!

Summary

In this chapter, we have seen how predictive models can be trained in Jupyter Notebooks.

To begin with, we talked about how to plan a machine learning strategy. We thought about how to design a plan that can lead to actionable business insights and stressed the importance of using the data to help set realistic business goals. We also explained machine learning terminology such as supervised learning, unsupervised learning, classification, and regression.

Next, we discussed methods for preprocessing data using scikit-learn and pandas. This included lengthy discussions and examples of a surprisingly time-consuming part of machine learning: dealing with missing data.

In the latter half of the chapter, we trained predictive classification models for our binary problem, comparing how decision boundaries are drawn for various models such as the SVM, k-Nearest Neighbors, and Random Forest. We then showed how validation curves can be used to make good parameter choices and how dimensionality reduction can improve model performance. Finally, at the end of our activity, we explored how the final model can be used in practice to make data-driven decisions.

In the next chapter, we will focus on data acquisition. Specifically, we will analyze HTTP requests, scrape tabular data from a web page, build and transform Pandas DataFrames, and finally create visualizations.

3

Web Scraping and Interactive Visualizations

Learning Objectives

By the end of this chapter, you will be able to:

- Describe how HTTP requests work
- Scrape tabular data from a web page
- Build and transform Pandas DataFrames
- Create interactive visualizations

In this chapter, you will learn the fundamentals of HTTP requests, scrape web page data, and then create interactive visualizations using the Jupyter Notebook.

Introduction

So far in this book, we have focused on using Jupyter to build reproducible data analysis pipelines and predictive models. We'll continue to explore these topics in this chapter, but the main focus here is data acquisition. In particular, we will show you how data can be acquired from the web using HTTP requests. This will involve scraping web pages by requesting and parsing HTML. We will then wrap up this chapter by using interactive visualization techniques to explore the data we've collected.

The amount of data available online is huge and relatively easy to acquire. It's also continuously growing and becoming increasingly important. Part of this continual growth is the result of an ongoing global shift from newspapers, magazines, and TV to online content. With customized newsfeeds available all the time on cell phones, and live-news sources such as Facebook, Reddit, Twitter, and YouTube, it's difficult to imagine the historical alternatives being relevant much longer. Amazingly, this accounts for only some of the increasingly massive amounts of data available online.

With this global shift toward consuming content using HTTP services (blogs, news sites, Netflix, and so on), there are plenty of opportunities to use data-driven analytics. For example, Netflix looks at the movies a user watches and predicts what they will like. This prediction is used to determine the suggested movies that appear. In this chapter, however, we won't be looking at "business-facing" data as such, but instead we will see how the client can leverage the internet as a database. Never before has this amount and variety of data been so easily accessible. We'll use web-scraping techniques to collect data, and then we'll explore it with interactive visualizations in Jupyter.

Interactive visualization is a visual form of data representation, which helps users understand the data using graphs or charts. Interactive visualization helps a developer or analyst present data in a simple form, which can be understood by non-technical personnel too.

Scraping Web Page Data

In the spirit of leveraging the internet as a database, we can think about acquiring data from web pages either by scraping content or by interfacing with web APIs. Generally, scraping content means getting the computer to read data that was intended to be displayed in a human-readable format. This is in contradistinction to web APIs, where data is delivered in machine-readable formats—the most common being JSON.

In this topic, we will focus on web scraping. The exact process for doing this will depend on the page and desired content. However, as we will see, it's quite easy to scrape anything we need from an HTML page so long as we have an understanding of the underlying concepts and tools. In this topic, we'll use Wikipedia as an example and scrape tabular content from an article. Then, we'll apply the same techniques to scrape data from a page on an entirely separate domain. But first, we'll take some time to introduce HTTP requests.

Introduction to HTTP Requests

The Hypertext Transfer Protocol, or HTTP for short, is the foundation of data communication for the internet. It defines how a page should be requested and how the response should look. For example, a client can request an Amazon page of laptops for sale, a Google search of local restaurants, or their Facebook feed. Along with the URL, the request will contain the user agent and available browsing cookies among the contents of the request header. The user agent tells the server what browser and device the client is using, which is usually used to provide the most user-friendly version of the web page's response. Perhaps they have recently logged in to the web page; such information would be stored in a cookie that might be used to automatically log the user in.

These details of HTTP requests and responses are taken care of under the hood thanks to web browsers. Luckily for us, today the same is true when making requests with high-level languages such as Python. For many purposes, the contents of request headers can be largely ignored. Unless otherwise specified, these are automatically generated in Python when requesting a URL. Still, for the purposes of troubleshooting and understanding the responses yielded by our requests, it's useful to have a foundational understanding of HTTP.

There are many types of HTTP methods, such as GET, HEAD, POST, and PUT. The first two are used for requesting that data be sent from the server to the client, whereas the last two are used for sending data to the server.

> **Note**
>
> Take a look at this GET request example for the **Profile** page on the site https://www.studytonight.com/. The exact page that was requested contains parameters, which start after the question mark (?) and are separated by the ampersands (&). These are usually used to modify the page specified by the path to source on the web server. In this case, the **User-Agent** is Mozilla/5.0, which corresponds to a standard desktop browser. Among other lines in the header, we note the **Accept** and **Accept-Language** fields, which specify the acceptable content types and language of the response.

These HTTP methods are summarized below:

- **GET**: Retrieves the information from the specified URL
- **HEAD**: Retrieves the meta information from the HTTP header of the specified URL
- **POST**: Sends the attached information for appending to the resource(s) at the specified URL
- **PUT**: Sends the attached information for replacing the resource(s) at the specified URL

A **GET** request is sent each time we type a web page address into our browser and press Enter. For web scraping, this is usually the only HTTP method we are interested in, and it's the only method we'll be using in this chapter.

Once the request has been sent, a variety of response types can be returned from the server. These are labeled with 100-level to 500-level codes, where the first digit in the code represents the response class. These can be described as follows:

- **1xx**: Informational response, for example, server is processing a request. It's uncommon to see this.
- **2xx**: Success, for example, page has loaded properly.
- **3xx**: Redirection, for example, the requested resource has been moved and we were redirected to a new URL.
- **4xx**: Client error, for example, the requested resource does not exist.
- **5xx**: Server error, for example, the website server is receiving too much traffic and could not fulfill the request.

For the purposes of web scraping, we usually only care about the response class, that is, the first digit of the response code. However, there exist subcategories of responses within each class that offer more granularity on what's going on. For example, a 401 code indicates an unauthorized response, whereas a 404 code indicates a page not found response. This distinction is noteworthy because a 404 would indicate we've requested a page that does not exist, whereas 401 tells us we need to log in to view the particular resource.

Let's see how HTTP requests can be done in Python and explore some of these topics using the Jupyter Notebook.

Making HTTP Requests in the Jupyter Notebook

Now that we've talked about how HTTP requests work and what type of responses we should expect, let's see how this can be done in Python. We'll use a library called **Requests**, which happens to be the most downloaded external library for Python. It's possible to use Python's built-in tools, such as `urllib`, for making HTTP requests, but **Requests** is far more intuitive, and in fact it's recommended over `urllib` in the official Python documentation.

Requests is a great choice for making simple and advanced web requests. It allows for all sorts of customization with respect to headers, cookies, and authorization. It tracks redirects and provides methods for returning specific page content such as JSON. Furthermore, there's an extensive suite of advanced features. However, it does not allow JavaScript to be rendered.

Oftentimes, servers return HTML with JavaScript code snippets included, which are automatically run in the browser on load time. When requesting content with Python using Requests, this JavaScript code is visible, but it does not run. Therefore, any elements that would be altered or created by doing so are missing. Often, this does not affect the ability to get the desired information, but in some cases we may need to render the JavaScript in order to scrape the page properly. For doing this, we could use a library like Selenium.

This has a similar API to the Requests library, but provides support for rendering JavaScript using web drivers. It can even run JavaScript commands on live pages, for example, to change the text color or scroll to the bottom of the page.

> **Note**
>
> For more information, refer to: http://docs.python-requests.org/en/master/user/advanced/ and http://selenium-python.readthedocs.io/.

Let's dive into an exercise using the Requests library with Python in a Jupyter Notebook.

Exercise 14: Handling HTTP Requests With Python in a Jupyter Notebook

1. Start the **NotebookApp** from the project directory by executing jupyter notebook. Navigate to the **lesson-3** directory and open up the **lesson- 3-workbook.ipynb** file. Find the cell near the top where the packages are loaded and run it.

    We are going to request a web page and then examine the response object. There are many different libraries for making requests and many choices for exactly how to do so with each. We'll only use the Requests library, as it provides excellent documentation, advanced features, and a simple API.

2. Scroll down to **Subtopic A: Introduction to HTTP requests** and run the first cell in that section to import the Requests library. Then, prepare a request by running the cell containing the following code:

```
url = 'https://jupyter.org/'
req = requests.Request('GET', url) req.headers['User-Agent'] =
'Mozilla/5.0'
req = req.prepare()
```

We use the Request class to prepare a GET request to the jupyter.org homepage. By specifying the user agent as Mozilla/5.0, we are asking for a response that would be suitable for a standard desktop browser. Finally, we prepare the request.

3. Print the docstring for the "prepared request" req, by running the cell containing **req?**:

```
In [83]:  req?

Type:         PreparedRequest
String form:  <PreparedRequest [GET]>
File:         ~/anaconda/lib/python3.5/site-packages/requests/models.py
Docstring:
The fully mutable :class:`PreparedRequest <PreparedRequest>` object,
containing the exact bytes that will be sent to the server.

Generated from either a :class:`Request <Request>` object or manually.

Usage::

  >>> import requests
  >>> req = requests.Request('GET', 'http://httpbin.org/get')
  >>> r = req.prepare()
  <PreparedRequest [GET]>

  >>> s = requests.Session()
  >>> s.send(r)
  <Response [200]>
```

Figure 3.1: Printing the docstring for req

Looking at its usage, we see how the request can be sent using a session. This is similar to opening a web browser (starting a session) and then requesting a URL.

4. Make the request and store the response in a variable named page, by running the following code:

```
with requests.Session() as sess: page = sess.send(req)
```

This code returns the HTTP response, as referenced by the page variable. By using the **with** statement, we initialize a session whose scope is limited to the indented code block. This means we do not have to worry about explicitly closing the session, as it is done automatically.

5. Run the next two cells in the notebook to investigate the response. The string representation of page should indicate a 200 status code response. This should agree with the **status_code** attribute.

6. Save the response text to the **page_html** variable and take a look at the head of the string with **page_html[:1000]**:

```
page_html = page.text
```

```
page_html[:1000]
```

```
'<!DOCTYPE html>\n<html>\n\n  <head>\n\n    <meta charset="utf-8">\n    <meta http-equiv="X-U
A-Compatible" content="IE=edge">\n    <meta name="viewport" content="width=device-width, init
ial-scale=1">\n    <meta name="description" content="">\n    <meta name="author" content="">\
n\n    <title>Project Jupyter | Home</title>\n    <meta property="og:title" content="Project
Jupyter" />\n    <meta property="og:description" content="The Jupyter Notebook is a web-based
interactive computing platform. The notebook combines live code, equations, narrative text, v
isualizations, interactive dashboards and other media.\n">\n    <meta property="og:url" conte
nt="http://www.jupyter.org" />\n    <meta property="og:image" content="http://jupyter.org/ass
ets/homepage.png" />\n    <!-- Bootstrap Core CSS -->\n    <script src="/cdn-cgi/apps/head/Mu
II141_IVFkxldaVulmdWee9as.js"></script><link rel="stylesheet" href="/css/bootstrap.min.css">\
n    <link rel="stylesheet" href="/css/logo-nav.css">\n    <link rel="stylesheet" href="/c'
```

Figure 3.2: The HTML response text

As expected, the response is HTML. We can format this output better with the help of **BeautifulSoup**, a library which will be used extensively for HTML parsing later in this section.

7. Print the head of the formatted HTML by running the following:

```
from bs4 import BeautifulSoup
print(BeautifulSoup(page_html, 'html.parser').prettify() [:1000])
```

We import **BeautifulSoup** and then print the output, where newlines are indented depending on their hierarchy in the HTML structure.

8. We can take this a step further and actually display the HTML in Jupyter by using the IPython display module. Do this by running the following code:

```
from IPython.display import HTML HTML(page_html)Here, we see the HTML
rendered as well as possible, given that no JavaScript code has been run
and no external resources have loaded. For example, the images that are
hosted on the jupyter.org server are not rendered and we instead see the
```
alt text: **circle of programming icons**, **Jupyter logo**, and so on.

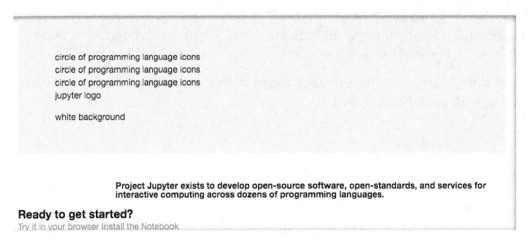

Figure 3.3: The output obtained when no images are loaded

9. Let's compare this to the live website, which can be opened in Jupyter using an IFrame. Do this by running the following code:

```
from IPython.display import IFrame IFrame(src=url, height=800, width=800)
```

Figure 3.4: Rendering of the entire Jupyter website

Here, we see the full site rendered, including JavaScript and external resources. In fact, we can even click on the hyperlinks and load those pages in the IFrame, just like a regular browsing session.

10. It's good practice to close the IFrame after using it. This prevents it from eating up memory and processing power. It can be closed by selecting the cell and clicking **Current Outputs | Clear** from the Cell menu in the Jupyter Notebook.

    Recall how we used a prepared request and session to request this content as a string in Python. This is often done using a shorthand method instead. The drawback is that we do not have as much customization of the request header, but that's usually fine.

11. Make a request to http://www.python.org/ by running the following code:

    ```
    url = 'http://www.python.org/' page = requests.get(url)
    page
    <Response [200]>
    ```

    The string representation of the page (as displayed beneath the cell) should indicate a 200 status code, indicating a successful response.

12. Run the next two cells. Here, we print the **url** and history attributes of our page.

    The URL returned is not what we input; notice the difference? We were redirected from the input URL, http://www.python.org/, to the secured version of that page, https://www.python.org/. The difference is indicated by an additional s at the start of the URL, in the protocol. Any redirects are stored in the history attribute; in this case, we find one page in here with status code 301 (permanent redirect), corresponding to the original URL requested.

Now that we're comfortable making requests, we'll turn our attention to parsing the HTML. This can be something of an art, as there are usually multiple ways to approach it, and the best method often depends on the details of the specific HTML in question.

Parsing HTML in the Jupyter Notebook

When scraping data from a web page, after making the request, we must extract the data from the response content. If the content is HTML, then the easiest way to do this is with a high-level parsing library such as Beautiful Soup. This is not to say it's the only way; in principle, it would be possible to pick out the data using regular expressions or Python string methods such as split, but pursuing either of these options would be an inefficient use of time and could easily lead to errors. Therefore, it's generally frowned upon and instead, the use of a trustworthy parsing tool is recommended.

In order to understand how content can be extracted from HTML, it's important to know the fundamentals of HTML. For starters, HTML stands for Hyper Text Markup Language. Like Markdown or XML (eXtensible Markup Language), it's simply a language for marking up text. In HTML, the display text is contained within the content section of HTML elements, where element attributes specify how that element should appear on the page.

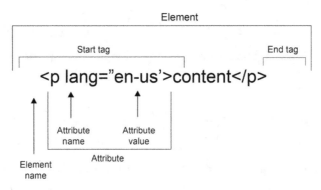

Figure 3.5: Fundamental blocks of HTML

Looking at the anatomy of an HTML element, as seen in the preceding picture, we see the content enclosed between start and end tags. In this example, the tags are **<p>** for paragraph; other common tag types are **<div>** (text block), **<table>** (data table),

<h1> (heading), **<img>** (image), and **<a>** (hyperlinks). Tags have attributes, which can hold important metadata. Most commonly, this metadata is used to specify how the element text should appear on the page. This is where CSS files come into play. The attributes can store other useful information, such as the hyperlink **href** in an **<a>** tag, which specifies a URL link, or the alternate alt label in an **<img>** tag, which specifies the text to display if the image resource cannot be loaded.

Now, let's turn our attention back to the Jupyter Notebook and parse some HTML! Although not necessary when following along with this exercise, it's very helpful in real-world situations to use the developer tools in Chrome or Firefox to help identify the HTML elements of interest. We'll include instructions for doing this with Chrome in the following exercise.

Exercise 15: Parsing HTML With Python in a Jupyter Notebook

1. In **lesson-3-workbook.ipynb** file, scroll to the top of **Subtopic B: Parsing HTML** with Python.

   In this exercise, we'll scrape the central bank interest rates for each country, as reported by Wikipedia. Before diving into the code, let's first open up the web page containing this data.

2. Go to https://en.wikipedia.org/wiki/List_of_countries_by_central_bank_interest_rates in a web browser. Use Chrome, if possible, as later in this exercise we'll show you how to view and search the HTML using Chrome's developer tools.

   Looking at the page, we see very little content other than a big list of countries and their interest rates. This is the table we'll be scraping.

3. Return to the Jupyter Notebook and load the HTML as a Beautiful Soup object so that it can be parsed. Do this by running the following code:

   ```
   from bs4 import BeautifulSoup
   soup = BeautifulSoup(page.content, 'html.parser')
   ```

   We use Python's default html.parser as the parser, but third-party parsers such as **lxml** may be used instead, if desired. Usually, when working with a new object like this Beautiful Soup one, it's a good idea to pull up the docstring by doing **soup?**. However, in this case, the docstring is not particularly informative. Another tool for exploring Python objects is **pdir**, which lists all of an object's attributes and methods (this can be installed with pip install **pdir2**). It's basically a formatted version of Python's built-in **dir** function.

4. Display the attributes and methods for the BeautifulSoup object by running the following code. This will run, regardless of whether or not the **pdir** external library is installed:

   ```
   try:
   import pdir dir = pdir
   except:
   print('You can install pdir with:\npip install pdir2') dir(soup)
   ```

   Here, we see a list of methods and attributes that can be called on soup. The most commonly used function is probably **find_all**, which returns a list of elements that match the given criteria.

5. Get the h1 heading for the page with the following code:

   ```
   h1 = soup.find_all('h1') h1
   >> [<h1 class="firstHeading" id="firstHeading" lang="en">List of countries
   by central bank interest rates</h1>]
   ```

   Usually, pages only have one H1 (top-level heading) element, so it's no surprise that we only find one here.

6. Run the next couple of cells. We redefine H1 to the first (and only) list element with **h1 = h1[0]**, and then print out the HTML element attributes with **h1.attrs**:

   We see the class and ID of this element, which can both be referenced by CSS code to define the style of this element.

7. Get the HTML element content (that is, the visible text) by printing **h1.text**.

8. Get all the images on the page by running the following code:

```
imgs = soup.find_all('img') len(imgs)
>> 91
```

There are lots of images on the page. Most of these are for the country flags.

9. Print the source of each image by running the following code:

```
[element.attrs['src'] for element in imgs if 'src' in element.attrs.
keys()]
```

We use a list comprehension to iterate through the elements, selecting the **src** attribute of each (so long as that attribute is actually available).

Now, let's scrape the table. We'll use Chrome's developer tools to hunt down the element this is contained within.

```
['//upload.wikimedia.org/wikipedia/commons/thumb/3/36/Flag_of_Albania.svg/21px-Flag_of_Albania.svg.png',
 '//upload.wikimedia.org/wikipedia/commons/thumb/9/9d/Flag_of_Angola.svg/23px-Flag_of_Angola.svg.png',
 '//upload.wikimedia.org/wikipedia/commons/thumb/1/1a/Flag_of_Argentina.svg/23px-Flag_of_Argentina.svg.png',
 '//upload.wikimedia.org/wikipedia/commons/thumb/2/2f/Flag_of_Armenia.svg/23px-Flag_of_Armenia.svg.png',
 '//upload.wikimedia.org/wikipedia/en/thumb/b/b9/Flag_of_Australia.svg/23px-Flag_of_Australia.svg.png',
 '//upload.wikimedia.org/wikipedia/commons/thumb/d/dd/Flag_of_Azerbaijan.svg/23px-Flag_of_Azerbaijan.svg.png',
 '//upload.wikimedia.org/wikipedia/commons/thumb/9/93/Flag_of_the_Bahamas.svg/23px-Flag_of_the_Bahamas.svg.png',
 '//upload.wikimedia.org/wikipedia/commons/thumb/2/2c/Flag_of_Bahrain.svg/23px-Flag_of_Bahrain.svg.png',
 '//upload.wikimedia.org/wikipedia/commons/thumb/f/f9/Flag_of_Bangladesh.svg/23px-Flag_of_Bangladesh.svg.png',
 '//upload.wikimedia.org/wikipedia/commons/thumb/e/ef/Flag_of_Barbados.svg/23px-Flag_of_Barbados.svg.png',
 '//upload.wikimedia.org/wikipedia/commons/thumb/8/85/Flag_of_Belarus.svg/23px-Flag_of_Belarus.svg.png',
 '//upload.wikimedia.org/wikipedia/commons/thumb/f/fa/Flag_of_Botswana.svg/23px-Flag_of_Botswana.svg.png',
 '//upload.wikimedia.org/wikipedia/en/thumb/0/05/Flag_of_Brazil.svg/22px-Flag_of_Brazil.svg.png',
 '//upload.wikimedia.org/wikipedia/commons/thumb/9/9a/Flag_of_Bulgaria.svg/23px-Flag_of_Bulgaria.svg.png',
```

Figure 3.6: Scraping the table on the target web page

10. If not already done, open the Wikipedia page we're looking at in Chrome. Then, in the browser, select **Developer Tools** from the **View** menu. A sidebar will open. The HTML is available to look at from the **Elements** tab in Developer Tools.

11. Select the little arrow in the top left of the tools sidebar. This allows us to hover over the page and see where the HTML element is located, in the **Elements** section of the sidebar:

Figure 3.7: Arrow Icon for locating the HTML element

12. Hover over the body to see how the table is contained within the div that has `id="bodyContent"`:

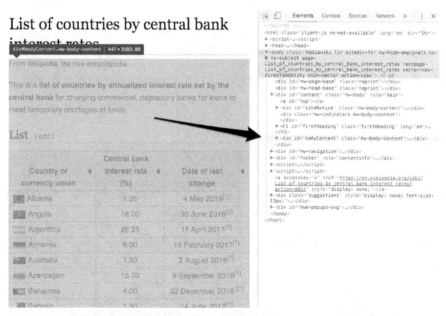

Figure 3.8: HTML code for table on the target web page

13. Select that **div** by running the following code:

```
body_content = soup.find('div', {'id': 'bodyContent'})
```

We can now seek out the table within this subset of the full HTML. Usually, tables are organized into headers **\<th\>**, rows **\<tr\>**, and data entries **\<td\>**.

14. Get the table headers by running the following code:

```
table_headers = body_content.find_all('th')[:3] table_headers
>>> [<th>Country or<br/>
currency union</th>, <th>Central bank<br/> interest rate (%)</th>,
<th>Date of last<br/> change</th>]
```

Here, we see three headers. In the content of each is a break element **\<br/\>**, which will make the text a bit more difficult to cleanly parse.

15. Get the text by running the following code:

```
table_headers = [element.get_text().replace('\n', ' ')
for element in table_headers]
table_headers
>> ['Country or currency union', 'Central bank interest rate (%)', 'Date
of last change']
```

Here, we get the content with the **get_text** method, and then run the replace string method to remove the newline resulting from the **\<br/\>** element.

To get the data, we'll first perform some tests and then scrape all the data in a single cell.

16. Get the data for each cell in the second **\<tr\>** (row) element by running the following code:

```
row_number = 2
d1, d2, d3 = body_content.find_all('tr')[row_number]\
.find_all('td')
```

We find all the row elements, pick out the third one, and then find the three data elements inside that.

Let's look at the resulting data and see how to parse the text from each row.

17. Run the next couple of cells to print **d1** and its text attribute:

```
d1

<td align="left"><span class="flagicon"><img alt="" class="thumbborder" data-file-height="300
" data-file-width="450" height="15" src="//upload.wikimedia.org/wikipedia/commons/thumb/9/9d/
Flag_of_Angola.svg/23px-Flag_of_Angola.svg.png" srcset="//upload.wikimedia.org/wikipedia/comm
ons/thumb/9/9d/Flag_of_Angola.svg/35px-Flag_of_Angola.svg.png 1.5x, //upload.wikimedia.org/wi
kipedia/commons/thumb/9/9d/Flag_of_Angola.svg/45px-Flag_of_Angola.svg.png 2x" width="23"/> </
span><a href="/wiki/Angola" title="Angola">Angola</a></td>
```

```
d1.text

'\xa0Angola'
```

Figure 3.9: Printing d1 and its text attribute

We're getting some undesirable characters at the front. This can be solved by searching for only the text of the **<a>** tag.

18. Run **d1.find('a').text** to return the properly *cleaned* data for that cell.

19. Run the next couple of cells to print **d2** and its text. This data appears to be clean enough to convert directly into a float.

20. Run the next couple of cells to print **d3** and its text:

```
d3

<td><span class="sortkey" style="display:none;speak:none">000000002016-06-30-0000</span><span
style="white-space:nowrap">30 June 2016</span><sup class="reference" id="cite_ref-CentralBank
News_1-1"><a href="#cite_note-CentralBankNews-1">[1]</a></sup></td>
```

```
d3.text

'000000002016-06-30-000030 June 2016[1]'
```

Figure 3.10: Printing d3 and its text attribute

Similar to **d1**, we see that it would be better to get only the span element's text.

21. Properly parse the date for this table entry by running the following code:

```
d3.find_all('span')[1].text
>> '30 June 2016'
```

22. Now, we're ready to perform the full scrape by iterating over the row elements `<th>`. Run the following code:

```
data = []
for i, row in enumerate(body_content.find_all('tr')):
...

...
>> Ignoring row 101 because len(data) != 3
>> Ignoring row 102 because len(data) != 3
```

> **Note**
>
> For the complete code, refer to the following: https://bit.ly/2EKMNbV.

We iterate over the rows, ignoring any that contain more than three data elements. These rows will not correspond to data in the table we are interested in. Rows that do have three data elements are assumed to be in the table, and we parse the text from these as identified during the testing.

The text parsing is done inside a **try/except** statement, which will catch any errors and allow this row to be skipped without stopping the iteration. Any rows that raise errors due to this statement should be looked at. The data for these could be recorded manually or accounted for by altering the scraping loop and re-running it. In this case, we'll ignore any errors for the sake of time.

23. Print the head of the scraped data list by running **print(data[:10])**:

```
>> [['Albania', 1.25, '4 May 2016'],
['Angola', 16.0, '30 June 2016'],
['Argentina', 26.25, '11 April 2017'],
['Armenia', 6.0, '14 February 2017'],
['Australia', 1.5, '2 August 2016'],
['Azerbaijan', 15.0, '9 September 2016'],
['Bahamas', 4.0, '22 December 2016'],
['Bahrain', 1.5, '14 June 2017'],
['Bangladesh', 6.75, '14 January 2016'],
['Belarus', 12.0, '28 June 2017']]
```

24. We'll visualize this data later in the chapter. For now, save the data to a CSV file by running the following code:

```
f_path = '../data/countries/interest-rates.csv' with open(f_path, 'w') as f:
f.write('{};{};{}\n'.format(*table_headers)) for d in data:
```

```
f.write('{};{};{}\n'.format(*d))
```

Note that we are using semicolons to separate the fields.

Activity 3: Web Scraping With Jupyter Notebooks

You should have completed the previous exercise in this chapter.

In this activity, we are going to get the population of each country. Then, in the next topic, this will be visualized along with the interest rate data scraped in the previous exercise.

The page we look at in this activity is available here: http://www.worldometers.info/world-population/population-by-country/.

Our aim is to apply the basic of web scrapping to a new web page and scrape some more data.

> **Note**
>
> This page may have changed since this document was created. If this URL no longer leads to a table of country populations, please use this Wikipedia page instead: https://en.wikipedia.org/wiki/List_of_countries_by_population(United_Nations).

In order to do this, the following steps have to be executed:

1. Scrape the data from the web page.

2. In the **lesson-3-workbook.ipynb** Jupyter Notebook, scroll to **Activity A: Web scraping with Python**.

3. Set the **url** variable and load an IFrame of our page in the notebook.

4. Close the IFrame by selecting the cell and clicking **Current Outputs** | Clear from the **Cell** menu in the Jupyter Notebook.

5. Request the page and load it as a **BeautifulSoup** object.

6. Print the H1 for the page.

7. Get and print the table headings.

8. Select first three columns and parse the text.

9. Get the data for a sample row.

10. How many columns of data do we have? Print the length of **row_data**.

11. Print the first elements of the row.

12. Select the data elements d1, d2, and d3.

13. Looking at the **row_data** output, we can find out how to correctly parse the data. Select the content of the **<a>** element in the first data element, and then simply get the text from the others.

14. Scrape and parse the table data.

15. Print the head of the scraped data.

16. Finally, save the data to a CSV file for later use.

> **Note**
>
> The detailed steps along with the solutions are presented in the *Appendix A* (pg. no. 160).

To summarize, we've seen how Jupyter Notebooks can be used for web scraping. We started this chapter by learning about HTTP methods and status codes. Then, we used the Requests library to actually perform HTTP requests with Python and saw how the Beautiful Soup library can be used to parse the HTML responses.

Our Jupyter Notebook turned out to be a great tool for this type of work. We were able to explore the results of our web requests and experiment with various HTML parsing techniques. We were also able to render the HTML and even load a live version of the web page inside the notebook!

In the next topic of this chapter, we shift to a completely new topic: interactive visualizations. We'll see how to create and display interactive charts right inside the notebook, and use these charts as a way to explore the data we have just collected.

Interactive Visualizations

Visualizations are quite useful as a means of extracting information from a dataset. For example, with a bar graph it's very easy to distinguish the value distribution, compared to looking at the values in a table. Of course, as we have seen earlier in this book, they can be used to study patterns in the dataset that would otherwise be quite difficult to identify. Furthermore, they can be used to help explain a dataset to an unfamiliar party. If included in a blog post, for example, they can boost reader interest levels and be used to break up blocks of text.

When thinking about interactive visualizations, the benefits are similar to static visualizations, but enhanced because they allow for active exploration on the viewer's part. Not only do they allow the viewer to answer questions they may have about the data, they also think of new questions while exploring. This can benefit a separate party such as a blog reader or co-worker, but also a creator, as it allows for easy ad hoc exploration of the data in detail, without having to change any code.

In this topic, we'll discuss and show how to use Bokeh to build interactive visualizations in Jupyter. Prior to this, however, we'll briefly revisit pandas DataFrames, which play an important role in doing data visualization with Python.

Building a DataFrame to Store and Organize Data

As we've seen time and time again in this book, pandas is an integral part of doing data science with Python and Jupyter Notebooks. DataFrames offer a way to organize and store labeled data, but more importantly, pandas provides time saving methods for transforming data within a DataFrame. Examples we have seen in this book include dropping duplicates, mapping dictionaries to columns, applying functions over columns, and filling in missing values.

With respect to visualizations, DataFrames offer methods for creating all sorts of matplotlib graphs, including `df.plot.barh()`, `df.plot.hist()`, and more. The interactive visualization library Bokeh previously relied on pandas DataFrames for their *high-level charts*. These worked similar to Seaborn, as we saw earlier in the previous chapter, where a DataFrame is passed to the plotting function along with the specific columns to plot. The most recent version of Bokeh, however, has dropped support for this behavior. Instead, plots are now created in much the same way as matplotlib, where the data can be stored in simple lists or NumPy arrays. The point of this discussion is that DataFrames are not entirely necessary, but still very helpful for organizing and manipulating the data prior to visualization.

Exercise 16: Building and Merging Pandas DataFrames

Let's dive right into an exercise, where we'll continue working on the country data we scraped earlier. Recall that we extracted the central bank interest rates and populations of each country, and saved the results in CSV files. We'll load the data from these files and merge them into a DataFrame, which will then be used as the data source for the interactive visualizations to follow.

1. In the `lesson-3-workbook.ipynb` of the Jupyter Notebook, scroll to the `Subtopic A: Building a DataFrame to store and organize data` subsection in the `Topic B` section.

We are first going to load the data from the CSV files, so that it's back to the state it was in after scraping. This will allow us to practice building DataFrames from Python objects, as opposed to using the **pd.read_csv** function.

> **Note**
>
> When using **pd.read_csv**, the datatype for each column will be inferred from the string input. On the other hand, when using **pd.DataFrame** as we do here, the datatype is instead taken as the type of the input variables. In our case, as will be seen, we read the file and do not bother converting the variables to numeric or date-time until after instantiating the DataFrame.

2. Load the CSV files into lists by running the following code:

```
with open('../data/countries/interest-rates.csv', 'r') as f:
int_rates_col_names = next(f).split(',')
int_rates = [line.split(',') for line in f.read(). splitlines()]
with open('../data/countries/populations.csv', 'r') as f: populations_col_
names = next(f).split(',')
populations = [line.split(',') for line in f.read(). splitlines()]
```

3. Check what the resulting lists look like by running the next two cells. We should see an output similar to the following:

```
print(int_rates_col_names) int_rates[:5]
>> ['Country or currency union', 'Central bank interest ...

...
['Indonesia', '263', '991', '379', '1.10 %'],
['Brazil', '209', '288', '278', '0.79 %']]
```

Now, the data is in a standard Python list structure, just as it was after scraping from the web pages in the previous sections. We're now going to create two DataFrames and merge them, so that all of the data is organized within one object.

4. Use the standard DataFrame constructor to create the two DataFrames by running the following code:

```
df_int_rates = pd.DataFrame(int_rates, columns=int_rates_ col_names)
df_populations = pd.DataFrame(populations, columns=populations_col_names)
```

This isn't the first time we've used this function in this book. Here, we pass the lists of data (as seen previously) and the corresponding column names. The input data can also be of dictionary type, which can be useful when each column is contained in a separate list.

Next, we're going to clean up each DataFrame. Starting with the interest rates one, let's print the head and tail, and list the data types.

5. When displaying the entire DataFrame, the default maximum number of rows is 60 (for version 0.18.1). Let's reduce this to 10 by running the following code:

```
pd.options.display.max_rows = 10
```

6. Display the head and tail of the interest rates DataFrame by running the following code:

df_int_rates

	Country or currency union	Central bank interest rate (%)	Date of last change
0	Albania	1.25	4 May 2016
1	Angola	16.0	30 June 2016
2	Argentina	26.25	11 April 2017
3	Armenia	6.0	14 February 2017
4	Australia	1.5	2 August 2016
...	...	...	...
84	United States	1.25	14 June 2017
85	Uzbekistan	9.0	1 January 2015
86	Vietnam	6.25	7 July 2017
87	West African States	3.5	16 September 2013
88	Zambia	12.5	17 May 2017

89 rows × 3 columns

Figure 3.11: Table for interest rates by country

7. Print the data types by running:

```
df_int_rates.dtypes
>> Country or currency union          object
>> Central bank interest rate (%)          object
>> Date of last change          object
>> dtype: object
```

Pandas has assigned each column as a string datatype, which makes sense because the input variables were all strings. We'll want to change these to string, float, and datetime, respectively.

8. Convert to the proper datatypes by running the following code:

```
df_int_rates['Central bank interest rate (%)'] = \ df_int_rates['Central
bank interest rate (%)']\
.astype(float, copy=False)
```

```
df_int_rates['Date of last change'] = \ pd.to_datetime(df_int_rates['Date
of last change'])
```

We use **astype** to cast the Interest Rate values as floats, setting **copy=False** to save memory. Since the date values are given in such an easy-to-read format, these can be converted simply by using **pd.to_datetime**.

9. Check the new datatypes of each column by running the following code:

```
df_int_rates.dtypes
>> Country or currency union                    object
>> Central bank interest rate (%)              float64
>> Date of last change                    datetime64[ns]
>> dtype: object
```

As can be seen, everything is now in the proper format.

10. Let's apply the same procedure to the other DataFrame. Run the next few cells to repeat the preceding steps for **df_populations**:

```
df_population
```

	Country (or dependency)	Population (2017)	Yearly Change
0	China	1,409,517,397	0.43 %
1	India	1,339,180,127	1.13 %
2	U.S.	324,459,463	0.71 %
3	Indonesia	263,991,379	1.10 %
4	Brazil	209,288,278	0.79 %
...	...	...	...
228	Saint Helena	4,049	0.35 %
229	Falkland Islands	2,910	0.00 %
230	Niue	1,618	-0.37 %
231	Tokelau	1,300	1.40 %
232	Holy See	792	-1.12 %

Figure 3.12: Table for population by country

Then, run this code:

```
df_populations['Population (2017)'] = df_populations['Population (2017)']\
.str.replace(',', '')\
.astype(float, copy=False)
df_populations['Yearly Change'] = df_populations['Yearly Change']\
.str.rstrip('%')\
.astype(float, copy=False)
```

To cast the numeric columns as a float, we had to first apply some modifications to the strings in this case. We stripped away any commas from the populations and removed the percent sign from the Yearly Change column, using string methods.

Now, we're going to merge the DataFrames on the country name for each row. Keep in mind that these are still the raw country names as scraped from the web, so there might be some work involved with matching the strings.

11. Merge the DataFrames by running the following code:

```
df_merge = pd.merge(df_populations,
df_int_rates,
left_on='Country (or dependency)', right_on='Country or currency union',
how='outer'
df_merge
```

We pass the population data in the left DataFrame and the interest rates in the right one, performing an outer match on the country columns. This will result in **NaN** values where the two do not overlap.

12. For the sake of time, let's just look at the most populated countries to see whether we missed matching any. Ideally, we would want to check everything. Look at the most populous countries by running the following code:

```
df_merge.sort_values('Population (2017)', ascending=False)\
.head(10)
```

	Country (or dependency)	Population (2017)	Yearly Change	Country or currency union	Central bank interest rate (%)	Date of last change
0	China	1.409517e+09	0.43	China	1.75	2015-10-23
1	India	1.339180e+09	1.13	India	6.00	2017-08-02
2	U.S.	3.244595e+08	0.71	NaN	NaN	NaT
3	Indonesia	2.639914e+08	1.10	Indonesia	4.75	2016-10-20
4	Brazil	2.092883e+08	0.79	Brazil	7.25	2017-07-26
5	Pakistan	1.970160e+08	1.97	Pakistan	5.75	2016-05-21
6	Nigeria	1.908863e+08	2.63	Nigeria	14.00	2016-07-26
7	Bangladesh	1.646698e+08	1.05	Bangladesh	6.75	2016-01-14
8	Russia	1.439898e+08	0.02	Russia	9.00	2017-06-16
9	Mexico	1.291633e+08	1.27	Mexico	7.00	2017-06-22

Figure 3.13: The table for most populous countries

It looks like U.S. didn't match up. This is because it's listed as *United States* in the interest rates data. Let's remedy this.

13. Fix the label for U.S. in the populations table by running the following code:

```
col = 'Country (or dependency)'
df_populations.loc[df_populations[col] == 'U.S.'] = 'United States'
```

We rename the country for the populations DataFrame with the use of the **loc** method to locate that row.

Now, let's merge the DataFrames properly.

14. Re-merge the DataFrames on the country names, but this time use an inner merge to remove the **NaN** values:

```
df_merge = pd.merge(df_populations,
df_int_rates,
left_on='Country (or dependency)', right_on='Country or currency union',
how='inner')
```

15. We are left with two identical columns in the merged DataFrame. Drop one of them by running the following code:

```
del df_merge['Country or currency union']
```

16. Rename the columns by running the following code:

```
name_map = {'Country (or dependency)': 'Country', 'Population (2017)':
'Population',
'Central bank interest rate (%)': 'Interest
rate'}
df_merge = df_merge.rename(columns=name_map)
```

We are left with the following merged and cleaned DataFrame:

	Country	Population	Yearly Change	Interest rate	Date of last change
0	China	1.409517e+09	0.43	1.75	2015-10-23
1	India	1.339180e+09	1.13	6.00	2017-08-02
2	United States	3.244595e+08	0.71	1.25	2017-06-14
3	Indonesia	2.639914e+08	1.10	4.75	2016-10-20
4	Brazil	2.092883e+08	0.79	7.25	2017-07-26
...	...	...	...	...	...
76	Mauritius	1.265138e+06	0.24	4.00	2016-07-20
77	Fiji	9.055020e+05	0.75	0.50	2011-11-02
78	Bahamas	3.953610e+05	1.06	4.00	2016-12-22
79	Iceland	3.350250e+05	0.77	4.50	2017-06-14
80	Samoa	1.964400e+05	0.67	0.14	2016-07-01

81 rows × 5 columns

Figure 3.14: Ouput after cleaning and merging tables

17. Now that we have all the data in a nicely organized table, we can move on to the fun part: visualizing it. Let's save this table to a CSV file for later use, and then move on to discuss how visualizations can be created with Bokeh.

    Write the merged data to a CSV file for later use with the following code:

    ```
    df_merge.to_csv('../data/countries/merged.csv', index=False)
    ```

Introduction to Bokeh

Bokeh is an interactive visualization library for Python. Its goal is to provide similar functionality to D3, the popular interactive visualization library for JavaScript. Bokeh functions very differently than D3, which is not surprising given the differences between Python and JavaScript. Overall, it's much simpler and it doesn't allow nearly as much customization as D3 does. This works to its advantage though, as it's much easier to use, and it still boasts an excellent suite of features that we'll explore in this section.

Let's dive right into a quick exercise with the Jupyter Notebook and introduce Bokeh by example.

> **Note**
>
> There is good documentation online for Bokeh, but much of it is outdated. Searching something like Bokeh bar plot in Google still tends to turn up documentation for legacy modules that no longer exist, for example, the high-level plotting tools that used to be available through **bokeh.charts** (prior to version 0.12.0). These are the ones that take pandas DataFrames as input in much the same way that Seaborn plotting functions do. Removing the high-level plotting tools module has simplified Bokeh, and will allow for more focused development going forward. Now, the plotting tools are largely grouped into the **bokeh. plotting** module, as will be seen in the next exercise and following activity.

Exercise 17: Introduction to Interactive Visualization With Bokeh

We'll load the required Bokeh modules and show some simple interactive plots that can be made with Bokeh. Please note that the examples in this book have been designed using version 0.12.10 of Bokeh.

1. In the **lesson-3-workbook.ipynb** Jupyter notebook, scroll to **Subtopic B: Introduction to Bokeh.**

2. Like scikit-learn, Bokeh modules are usually loaded in pieces (unlike pandas, for example, where the whole library is loaded at once). Import some basic plotting modules by running the following code:

   ```
   from bokeh.plotting import figure, show, output_notebook output_notebook()
   ```

   We need to run **output_notebook()** in order to render the interactive visuals within the Jupyter notebook.

3. Generate random data to plot by running the following code:

```
np.random.seed(30)
data = pd.Series(np.random.randn(200),
index=list(range(200)))\
.cumsum() x = data.index
y = data.values
```

The random data is generated using the cumulative sum of a random set of numbers that are distributed about zero. The effect is a trend that looks similar to a stock price time series, for example.

4. Plot the data with a line plot in Bokeh by running the following code:

```
p = figure(title='Example plot', x_axis_label='x', y_axis_ label='y')
p.line(x, y, legend='Random trend') show(p)
```

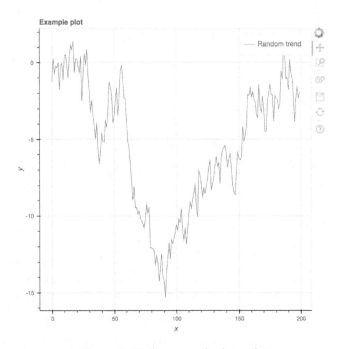

Figure 3.15: An example data plot

We instantiate the figure, as referenced by the variable **p**, and then plot a line. Running this in Jupyter yields an interactive figure with various options along the right-hand side.

The top three options (as of version 0.12.10) are **Pan**, **Box Zoom**, and **Wheel Zoom**. Play around with these and experiment with how they work. Use the reset option to re-load the default plot limits.

5. Other plots can be created with the alternative methods of **figure**. Draw a scatter plot by running the following code, where we replace **line** in the preceding code with **circle**:

```
size = np.random.rand(200) * 5
p = figure(title='Example plot', x_axis_label='x', y_axis_ label='y')
p.circle(x, y, radius=size, alpha=0.5, legend='Random dots')
show(p)
```

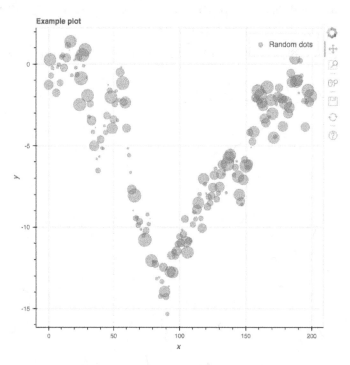

Figure 3.16: An example scatter plot

Here, we've specified the size of each circle using a random set of numbers. A very enticing feature of interactive visualizations is the tooltip. This is a hover tool that allows the user to get information about a point by hovering over it.

6. In order to add this tool, we're going to use a slightly different method for creating the plot. This will require us to import a couple of new libraries. Run the following code:

```
from bokeh.plotting import ColumnDataSource from bokeh.models import HoverTool
```

This time, we'll create a data source to pass to the plotting method. This can contain metadata, which can be included in the visualization via the hover tool.

7. Create random labels and plot the interactive visualization with a hover tool by running the following code:

```
source = ColumnDataSource(data=dict( x=x,
y=y,
...
...
source=source,
legend='Random dots')
show(p)
```

> **Note**
>
> For the complete code, refer to the following: https://bit.ly/2RhpU1r.

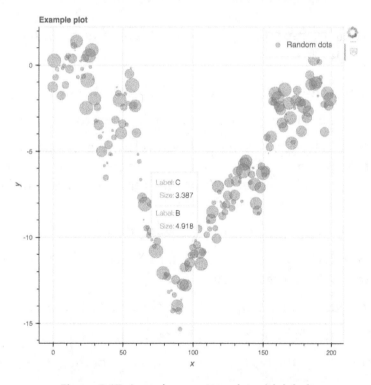

Figure 3.17: A random scatter plot with labels

We define a data source for the plot by passing a dictionary of key/value pairs to the **ColumnDataSource** constructor. This source includes the x location, y location, and size of each point, along with the random letter **A**, **B**, or **C** for each point. These random letters are assigned as labels for the hover tool, which will also display the size of each point. The **Hover Tool** is then added to the figure, and the data is retrieved from each element through the specific plotting method, which is circle in this case. The result is that we are now able to hover over the points and see the data we've selected for the **Hover Tool**! We notice, by looking at the toolbar to the right of the plot, that by explicitly including the **Hover Tool**, the others have disappeared. These can be included by manually adding them to the list of tool objects that gets passed to `bokeh.plotting.figure`.

8. Add pan, zoom, and reset tools to the plot by running the following code:

```
from bokeh.models import PanTool, BoxZoomTool, WheelZoomTool, ResetTool
...

...
legend='Random dots')
show(p)
```

This code is identical to what was previously shown except for the `tools` variable, which now references several new tools we've imported from the Bokeh library.

We'll stop the introductory exercise here, but we'll continue creating and exploring plots in the following activity.

Activity 4: Exploring Data with Interactive Visualizations

You should have completed the previous exercise in order to complete this activity.

We'll pick up using Bokeh right where we left off with the previous exercise, except instead of using the randomly generated data seen there, we'll instead use the data we scraped from the web in the first part of this chapter. Our aim is to use Bokeh to create interactive visualizations of our scraped data.

In order to do so, we need to execute the following steps:

1. In the **lesson-3-workbook.ipynb** file, scroll to the **Activity B: Interactive visualizations with Bokeh** section.

2. Load the previously scraped, merged, and cleaned web page data

3. Recall what the data looks like by displaying the DataFrame.

4. Draw a scatter plot of the population as a function of the interest rate.

5. In the data, we see some clear outliers with high populations. Hover over these to see what they are. Select the Box Zoom tool and alter the viewing window to better see the majority of the data.

6. Some of the lower population countries appear to have negative interest rates. Select the **Wheel Zoom** tool and use it to zoom in on this region. Use the **Pan** tool to re-center the plot, if needed, so that the negative interest rate samples are in view. Hover over some of these and see what countries they correspond to.

7. Add a **Year of last change** column to the DataFrame and add a color based on the date of last interest rate change

8. Create a map to group the last change date into color categories.

9. Create the colored visualization.

10. Looking for patterns, zoom in on the lower population countries.

11. Plot the interest rate as a function of the year-over-year population change by running the following code.

12. Determine the line of best fit for the previously plotted relationship.

13. Re-plot the output obtained in the preceding step and add a line of best fit.

14. Explore the plot by using the zoom tools and hovering over interesting samples.

> **Note**
>
> The detailed steps along with the solutions are presented in the *Appendix A* (pg. no. 163).

Summary

In this chapter, we scraped web page tables and then used interactive visualizations to study the data.

We started by looking at how HTTP requests work, focusing on GET requests and their response status codes. Then, we went into the Jupyter Notebook and made HTTP requests with Python using the Requests library. We saw how Jupyter can be used to render HTML in the notebook, along with actual web pages that can be interacted with. After making requests, we saw how Beautiful Soup can be used to parse text from the HTML, and used this library to scrape tabular data.

After scraping two tables of data, we stored them in pandas DataFrames. The first table contained the central bank interest rates for each country and the second table contained the populations. We combined these into a single table that was then used to create interactive visualizations.

Finally, we used Bokeh to render interactive visualizations in Jupyter. We saw how to use the Bokeh API to create various customized plots and made scatter plots with specific interactive abilities such as zoom, pan, and hover. In terms of customization, we explicitly showed how to set the point radius and color for each data sample.

Furthermore, when using Bokeh to explore the scraped population data, the tooltip was utilized to show country names and associated data when hovering over the points.

Congratulations for completing this introductory course on data science using Jupyter Notebooks! Regardless of your experience with Jupyter and Python coming into the book, you've learned some useful and applicable skills for practical data science!

Before finishing up, let's quickly recap the topics we've covered in this book.

The first chapter was an introduction to the Jupyter Notebook platform, where we covered all of the fundamentals. We learned about the interface and how to use and install magic functions. Then, we introduced the Python libraries we'll be using and walked through an exploratory analysis of the *Boston housing* dataset.

In the second chapter, we focused on doing machine learning with Jupyter. We first discussed the steps for developing a predictive analytics plan, and then looked at a few different types of models including SVM, a KNN classifier, and Random Forests.

Working with an *employee retention* dataset, we applied data cleaning methods and then trained models to predict whether an employee has left or not. We also explored more advanced topics such as overfitting, k-fold cross-validation, and validation curves.

Finally, in the third chapter, we shifted briefly from data analysis to data collection using web scraping and saw how to make HTTP requests and parse the HTML responses in Jupyter. Then, we finished up the book by using interactive visualizations to explore our collected data.

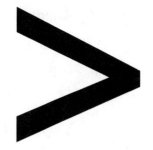

Appendix A

About

This section is included to assist the students to perform the activities present in the book. It includes detailed steps that are to be performed by the students to complete and achieve the objectives of the activity.

Chapter 1: Jupyter Fundamentals

Activity 1: Building a Third-Order Polynomial Model

1. Scroll to the empty cells at the bottom of **Subtopic C** in your Jupyter Notebook.

2. These will be found beneath the linear-model **MSE** calculation cell under the **Activity** heading.

> **Note**
>
> You should fill these empty cells in with code as we complete the activity. You may need to insert new cells as these become filled up; please do so as needed.

3. We will first pull out our dependent feature from and target variable from **df**. using the following:

   ```
   y = df['MEDV'].values
   x = df['LSTAT'].values.reshape(-1,1)
   ```

   This is identical to what we did earlier for the linear model.

4. Verify what **x** looks like by printing the first few samples with **print(x[:3])**:

   ```
   print('x =')
   print(x[:3], '...etc')
   ```

   ```
   x =
   [[ 4.98]
    [ 9.14]
    [ 4.03]] ...etc
   ```

   Figure 1.49: Printing first three values of x using print()

   Notice how each element in the array is itself an array with length 1. This is what **reshape(-1,1)** does, and it is the form expected by scikit-learn.

5. Transform **x** into "polynomial features" by importing the appropriate transformation tool from scikit-learn and instantiating the third-degree polynomial feature transformer:

   ```
   from sklearn.preprocessing import PolynomialFeatures poly =
   PolynomialFeatures(degree=3)
   ```

The rationale for this step may not be immediately obvious but will be explained shortly.

6. Transform the **LSTAT** feature (as stored in the variable **x**) by running the **fit_transform** method. Build the polynomial feature set by running the following code:

```
x_poly = poly.fit_transform(x)
```

Here, we have used the instance of the transformer feature to transform the LSTAT variable.

7. Verify what **x_poly** looks like by printing the first few samples with **print(x_poly[:3])**.

```
print('x_poly =')
print(x_poly[:3], '...etc')
```

```
x_poly =
[[   1.          4.98       24.8004     123.505992]
 [   1.          9.14       83.5396     763.551944]
 [   1.          4.03       16.2409      65.450827]] ...etc
```

Figure 1.50: Printing first three values of x_poly using print()

Unlike x, the arrays in each row now have length 4, where the values have been calculated as x^0, x^1, x^2 and x^3.

We are now going to use this data to fit a linear model. Labeling the features as a, b, c, and d, we will calculate the coefficients α_0, α_1, α_2, and α_3 and of the linear model:

$$y = \alpha_0 a + \alpha_1 b + \alpha_2 c + \alpha_3 d$$

We can plug in the definitions of a, b, c, and d, to get the following polynomial model, where the coefficients are the same as the previous ones:

$$y = \alpha_0 + \alpha_1 x + \alpha_2 x^2 + \alpha_3 x^3$$

8. Import the **LinearRegression** class and build our linear classification model the same way as done while calculating the MSE. Run the following:

```
from sklearn.linear_model import LinearRegression clf =
LinearRegression()
clf.fit(x_poly, y)
```

9. Extract the coefficients and print the polynomial model using the following code:

```
a_0 = clf.intercept_ + clf.coef_[0] # intercept
a_1, a_2, a_3 = clf.coef_[1:]        # other coefficients

msg = 'model: y = {:.3f} + {:.3f}x + {:.3f}x^2 + {:.3f}x^3'\
        .format(a_0, a_1, a_2, a_3)
print(msg)
```

```
msg = 'model: y = {:.3f} + {:.3f}x + {:.3f}x^2 + {:.3f}x^3'\
        .format(x_0, x_1, x_2, x_3)
print(msg)

model: y = 48.650 + -3.866x + 0.149x^2 + -0.002x^3
```

Figure 1.51: Extracting coefficients and printing the polynomial model

To get the actual model intercept, we have to add the **intercept_** and **coef_ [0]** attributes. The higher-order coefficients are then given by the remaining values of **coef_**.

10. Determine the predicted values for each sample and calculate the residuals by running the following code:

```
y_pred = clf.predict(x_poly) resid_MEDV = y - y_pred
```

11. Print some of the residual values by running **print(resid_MEDV[:10])**:

```
print('residuals =')
print(resid_MEDV[:10], '...etc')

residuals =
[ -8.84025736  -2.61360313  -0.65577837  -5.11949581   4.23191217
  -3.56387056   3.16728909  12.00336372   4.03348935   2.87915437] ...etc
```

Figure 1.52: Printing residual values

We'll plot these soon to compare with the linear model residuals, but first we will calculate the MSE.

12. Run the following code to print the MSE for the third-order polynomial model:

```
from sklearn.metrics import mean_squared_error error = mean_squared_
error(y, y_pred) print('mse = {:.2f}'.format(error))
```

```
error = mean_squared_error(y, y_pred)
print('mse = {:.2f}'.format(error))

mse = 28.88
```

Figure 1.53: Calculating the mean squared error

As can be seen, the **MSE** is significantly less for the polynomial model compared to the linear model (which was 38.5). This error metric can be converted to an average error in dollars by taking the square root. Doing this for the polynomial model, we find the average error for the median house value is only $5,300.

Now, we'll visualize the model by plotting the polynomial line of best fit along with the data.

13. Plot the polynomial model along with the samples by running the following:

```
fig, ax = plt.subplots() # Plot the samples
ax.scatter(x.flatten(), y, alpha=0.6)
# Plot the polynomial model
x_ = np.linspace(2, 38, 50).reshape(-1, 1) x_poly = poly.fit_transform(x_)
y_ = clf.predict(x_poly)
ax.plot(x_, y_, color='red', alpha=0.8) ax.set_xlabel('LSTAT'); ax.set_
ylabel('MEDV');
```

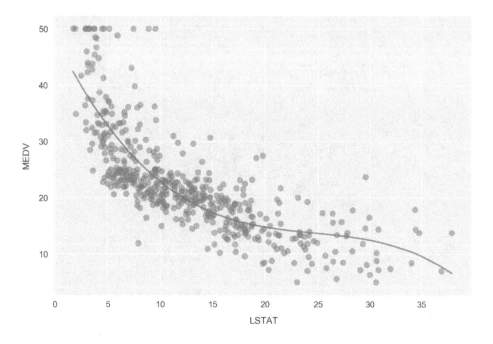

Figure 1.54: Plotting the polynomial model for MEDV and LSTAT

Here, we are plotting the red curve by calculating the polynomial model predictions on an array of **x** values. The array of **x** values was created using **np.linspace**, resulting in 50 values arranged evenly between 2 and 38.

Now, we'll plot the corresponding residuals. Whereas we used Seaborn for this earlier, we'll have to do it manually to show results for a scikit-learn model. Since we already calculated the residuals earlier, as reference by the **resid_MEDV** variable, we simply need to plot this list of values on a scatter chart.

14. Plot the residuals by running the following:

```
fig, ax = plt.subplots(figsize=(5, 7)) ax.scatter(x, resid_MEDV, alpha=0.6)
ax.set_xlabel('LSTAT')
ax.set_ylabel('MEDV Residual $(y-\hat{y})$') plt.axhline(0, color='black',
ls='dotted');
```

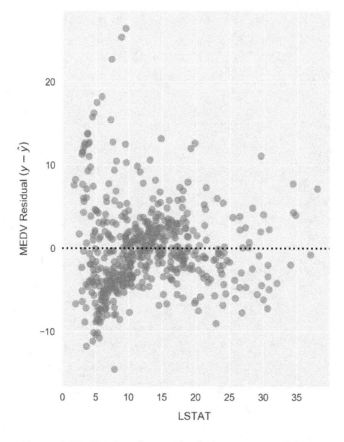

Figure 1.55: Plotting the residuals for LSTAT and MEDV

Compared to the linear model **LSTAT** residual plot, the polynomial model residuals appear to be more closely clustered around $y - \hat{y} = 0$. Note that y is the sample **MEDV** and $\hat{y}$ is the predicted value. There are still clear patterns, such as the cluster near $x = 7$ and $y = -7$ that indicates suboptimal modeling.

Having successfully modeled the data using a polynomial model, let's finish up this chapter by looking at categorical features. In particular, we are going to build a set of categorical features and use them to explore the dataset in more detail.

Chapter 2: Data Cleaning and Advanced Machine

Activity 2: Preparing to Train a Predictive Model for the Employee-Retention Problem

1. Scroll to the **Activity A** section of the **lesson-2-workbook.ipynb** notebook file.

2. Check the head of the table by running the following code:

   ```
   %%bash
   head ../data/hr-analytics/hr_data.csv
   ```

   Judging by the output, convince yourself that it looks to be in standard CSV format. For CSV files, we should be able to simply load the data with pd.read_csv.

3. Load the data with Pandas by running **df = pd.read_csv('../data/hr- analytics/ hr_data.csv')**. Write it out yourself and use tab completion to help type the file path.

4. Inspect the columns by printing **df.columns** and make sure the data has loaded as expected by printing the DataFrame **head** and **tail** with **df.head()** and **df.tail()**:

```
df.columns
```
```
Index(['satisfaction_level', 'last_evaluation', 'number_project',
       'average_montly_hours', 'time_spend_company', 'work_accident', 'left',
       'promotion_last_5years', 'is_smoker', 'department', 'salary'],
      dtype='object')
```
```
df.head()
```

	satisfaction_level	last_evaluation	number_project	average_montly_hours	time_spend_company	work_accident	left	promotio
0	0.38	0.53	2	157.0	3.0	0	yes	
1	0.80	0.86	5	262.0	6.0	0	yes	
2	0.11	0.88	7	272.0	4.0	0	yes	
3	0.72	0.87	5	223.0	5.0	0	yes	
4	0.37	0.52	2	NaN	NaN	0	yes	

```
df.tail()
```

	satisfaction_level	last_evaluation	number_project	average_montly_hours	time_spend_company	work_accident	left	pron
14994	0.40	0.57	2	151.0	3.0	0	yes	
14995	0.37	0.48	2	160.0	3.0	0	yes	
14996	0.37	0.53	2	143.0	3.0	0	yes	
14997	0.11	0.96	6	280.0	4.0	0	yes	
14998	0.37	0.52	2	158.0	3.0	0	yes	

Figure 2.45: Output for inspecting head and tail of columns

We can see that it appears to have loaded correctly. Based on the tail index values, there are nearly 15,000 rows; let's make sure we didn't miss any.

5. Check the number of rows (including the header) in the CSV file with the following code:

    ```
    with open('../data/hr-analytics/hr_data.csv') as f: print(len(f.read().
    splitlines()))
    ```

    ```
    # How many lines in the CSV (including header)

    with open('../data/hr-analytics/hr_data.csv') as f:
        print(len(f.read().splitlines()))
    ```
    ```
    15000
    ```

    Figure 2.46: Output after checking for number of rows

6. Compare this result to **len(df)** to make sure you've loaded all the data:

    ```
    # How many samples did we load into Python?

    len(df)
    ```
    ```
    14999
    ```

    Figure 2.47: Output after checking for number of sample uploaded

Now that our client's data has been properly loaded, let's think about how we can use predictive analytics to find insights into why their employees are leaving.

Let's run through the first steps for creating a predictive analytics plan:

Look at the available data: You've already done this by looking at the columns, datatypes, and the number of samples.

Determine the business needs: The client has clearly expressed their needs: reduce the number of employees who leave.

Assess the data for suitability: Let's try to determine a plan that can help satisfy the client's needs, given the provided data

Recall, as mentioned earlier, that effective analytics techniques lead to impactful business decisions. With that in mind, if we were able to predict how likely an employee is to quit, the business could selectively target those employees for special treatment. For example, their salary could be raised or their number of projects reduced. Furthermore, the impact of these changes could be estimated using the model!

To assess the validity of this plan, let's think about our data. Each row represents an employee who either works for the company or has left, as labeled by the column named left. We can therefore train a model to predict this target, given a set of features.

7. Assess the target variable. Check the distribution and number of missing entries by running the following code:

```
df.left.value_counts().plot('barh') print(df.left.isnull().sum()
```

```
# How is it distributed?

fig, ax = plt.subplots(figsize=(5, 3))
df.left.value_counts().plot('barh');
```

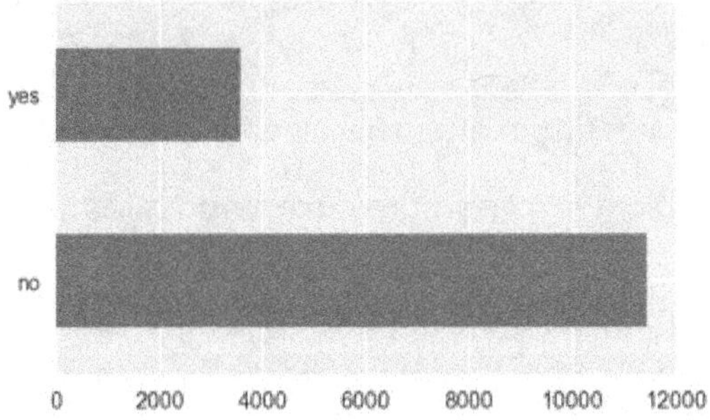

Figure 2.48: Distribution of the target variables

Here's the output of the second code line:

```
# How much missing data?

df.left.isnull().sum()

0
```

Figure 2.49: Output to check missing data points

About three-quarters of the samples are employees who have not left. The group that has left make up the other quarter of the samples. This tells us we are dealing with an imbalanced classification problem, which means we'll have to take special measures to account for each class when calculating accuracies. We also see that none of the target variables are missing (no NaN values).

Now, we'll assess the features:

8. Print the datatype of each by executing **df.dtypes**. Observe how we have a mix of continuous and discrete features:

```
# Print datatypes

df.dtypes
```

```
satisfaction_level         float64
last_evaluation            float64
number_project               int64
average_montly_hours       float64
time_spend_company         float64
work_accident                int64
left                        object
promotion_last_5years        int64
is_smoker                   object
department                  object
salary                      object
dtype: object
```

Figure 2.50: Printing data types for verification

9. Display the feature distributions by running the following code:

```
for f in df.columns: try:
fig = plt.figure()

...

...

print('-'*30)
```

> **Note**
>
> For the complete code, refer to the following: https://bit.ly/2D3iKL2.

This code snippet is a little complicated, but it's very useful for showing an overview of both the continuous and discrete features in our dataset. Essentially, it assumes each feature is continuous and attempts to plot its distribution, and reverts to simply plotting the value counts if the feature turns out to be discrete.

The result is as follows:

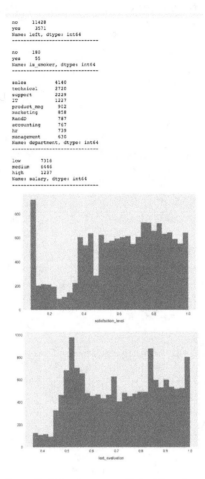

Figure 2.51: Distribution of all features: satisfaction_level and last_evaluation

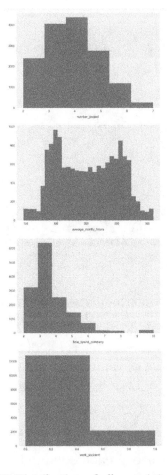

Figure 2.52: Distribution of all remaining features

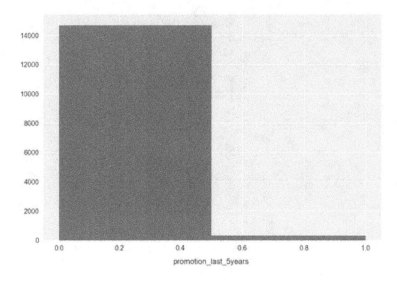

Figure 2.53: Distribution for the variable promotion_last_5years

For many features, we see a wide distribution over the possible values, indicating a good variety in the feature spaces. This is encouraging; features that are strongly grouped around a small range of values may not be very informative for the model. This is the case for **promotion_last_5years**, where we see that the vast majority of samples are **0**.

The next thing we need to do is remove any **NaN** values from the dataset.

10. Check how many **NaN** values are in each column by running the following code:

```
df.isnull().sum() / len(df) * 100
```

```
# How many NaNs?

df.isnull().sum() / len(df) * 100

satisfaction_level       0.000000
last_evaluation          0.000000
number_project           0.000000
average_montly_hours     2.453497
time_spend_company       1.006734
work_accident            0.000000
left                     0.000000
promotion_last_5years    0.000000
is_smoker               98.433229
department               0.000000
salary                   0.000000
dtype: float64
```

Figure 2.54: Verification for the number of NaN values

We can see there are about 2.5% missing for **average_montly_hours**, 1% missing for **time_spend_company**, and 98% missing for **is_smoker**! Let's use a couple of different strategies that you've learned to handle these.

11. Drop the **is_smoker** column as there is barely any information in this metric. Do this by running: **del df['is_smoker']**.

12. Fill the **NaN** values in the **time_spend_company** column. This can be done with the following code:

```
fill_value = df.time_spend_company.median()
df.time_spend_company = df.time_spend_company.fillna(fill_ value)
```

The final column to deal with is **average_montly_hours**. We could do something similar and use the median or rounded mean as the integer fill value. Instead though, let's try to take advantage of its relationship with another variable. This may allow us to fill the missing data more accurately.

13. Make a boxplot of **average_montly_hours** segmented by **number_project**. This can be done by running the following code:

```
sns.boxplot(x='number_project', y='average_montly_hours', data=df)
```

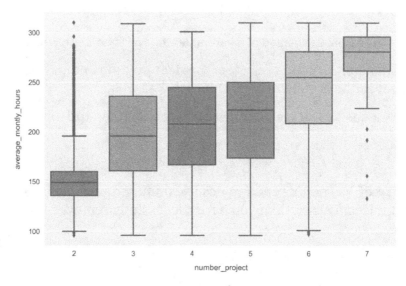

Figure 2.55: Boxplot for average_monthly_hours and number_project

We can see how the number of projects is correlated with **average_ monthly_hours**, a result that is hardly surprising. We'll exploit this relationship by filling in the **NaN** values of **average_montly_hours** differently, depending on the number of projects for that sample.

Specifically, we'll use the mean of each group.

14. Calculate the mean of each group by running the following code:

```
mean_per_project = df.groupby('number_project')\
.average_montly_hours.mean() mean_per_project = dict(mean_per_project)
print(mean_per_project)
```

```
# Calculate fill values for average_montly_hours

mean_per_project = df.groupby('number_project')\
                      .average_montly_hours.mean()
mean_per_project = dict(mean_per_project)
mean_per_project

{2: 160.16353543979506,
 3: 197.47882323104236,
 4: 205.07858315740089,
 5: 211.99962839093274,
 6: 238.73947368421054,
 7: 276.01587301587301}
```

Figure 2.56: Calculation of mean values for average_monthly_hours

We can then map this onto the **number_project** column and pass the resulting series object as the argument to **fillna**.

15. Fill the **NaN** values in **average_montly_hours** by executing the following code:

```
fill_values = df.number_project.map(mean_per_project)
df.average_montly_hours = df.average_montly_hours. fillna(fill_values)
```

16. Confirm that **df** has no more **NaN** values by running the following assertion test. If it does not raise an error, then you have successfully removed the **NaNs** from the table:

```
assert df.isnull().sum().sum() == 0
```

Note

We pass **index=False** so that the index is not written to file. In this case, the index is a set of integers spanning from 0 to the DataFrame length, and it therefore tells us nothing important.

17. Transform the string and Boolean fields into integer representations. In particular, we'll manually convert the target variable **left** from **yes** and **no** to **1** and **0** and build the one-hot encoded features. Do this by running the following code:

```
df.left = df.left.map({'no': 0, 'yes': 1}) df = pd.get_dummies(df)
```

18. Print **df.columns** to show the fields:

```
df.columns
Index(['satisfaction_level', 'last_evaluation', 'number_project',
       'average_montly_hours', 'time_spend_company', 'work_accident', 'left',
       'promotion_last_5years', 'department_IT', 'department_RandD',
       'department_accounting', 'department_hr', 'department_management',
       'department_marketing', 'department_product_mng', 'department_sales',
       'department_support', 'department_technical', 'salary_high',
       'salary_low', 'salary_medium'],
      dtype='object')
```

Figure 2.57: A screenshot of the different fields in the dataframe

We can see that department and salary have been split into various binary features.

The final step to prepare our data for machine learning is scaling the features, but for various reasons (for example, some models do not require scaling), we'll do it as part of the model-training workflow in the next activity.

19. We have completed the data preprocessing and are ready to move on to training models! Let's save our preprocessed data by running the following code:

```
df.to_csv('../data/hr-analytics/hr_data_processed.csv', index=False)
```

Chapter 3: Web Scraping and Interactive Visualizations

Activity 3: Web Scraping with Jupyter Notebooks

1. For this page, the data can be scraped using the following code snippet:

```
data = []
for i, row in enumerate(soup.find_all('tr')): row_data = row.find_all('td')
try:
d1, d2, d3 = row_data[1], row_data[5], row_data[6] d1 = d1.find('a').text
d2 = float(d2.text)
d3 = d3.find_all('span')[1].text.replace('+', '') data.append([d1, d2, d3])
except:
print('Ignoring row {}'.format(i)
```

2. In the **lesson-3-workbook.ipynb** Jupyter Notebook, scroll to **Activity A: Web scraping with Python**.

3. Set the **url** variable and load an IFrame of our page in the notebook by running the following code:

```
url = 'http://www.worldometers.info/world-population/ population-by-
country/'
IFrame(url, height=300, width=800)
```

The page should load in the notebook. Scrolling down, we can see the **Countries in the world by population** heading and the table of values beneath it. We'll scrape the first three columns from this table to get the countries, populations, and yearly population changes.

4. Close the IFrame by selecting the cell and clicking **Current Outputs | Clear** from the **Cell** menu in the Jupyter Notebook.

5. Request the page and load it as a **BeautifulSoup** object by running the following code:

```
page = requests.get(url)
soup = BeautifulSoup(page.content, 'html.parser')
```

We feed the page content to the **BeautifulSoup** constructor. Recall that previously, we used **page.text** here instead. The difference is that **page.content** returns the raw binary response content, whereas **page.text** returns the UTF-8 decoded content. It's usually best practice to pass the bytes object and let **BeautifulSoup** decode it, rather than doing it with Requests using **page.text**.

6. Print the H1 for the page by running the following code:

```
soup.find_all('h1')
>> [<h1>Countries in the world by population (2017)</h1>]
```

We'll scrape the table by searching for **\<th>**, **\<tr>**, and **\<td>** elements, as in the previous exercise.

7. Get and print the table headings by running the following code:

```
table_headers = soup.find_all('th') table_headers
>> [<th>#</th>,
<th>Country (or dependency)</th>,
<th>Population<br/> (2017)</th>,
<th>Yearly<br/> Change</th>,
<th>Net<br/> Change</th>,
<th>Density<br/> (P/Km²)</th>,
<th>Land Area<br/> (Km²)</th>,
<th>Migrants<br/> (net)</th>,
<th>Fert.<br/> Rate</th>,
<th>Med.<br/> Age</th>,
<th>Urban<br/> Pop %</th>,
<th>World<br/> Share</th>]
```

8. We are only interested in the first three columns. Select these and parse the text with the following code:

```
table_headers = table_headers[1:4] table_headers = [t.text.replace('\n',
'') for t in table_ headers]
```

After selecting the subset of table headers we want, we parse the text content from each and remove any newline characters.

Now, we'll get the data. Following the same prescription as the previous exercise, we'll test how to parse the data for a sample row.

9. Get the data for a sample row by running the following code:

```
row_number = 2
row_data = soup.find_all('tr')[row_number]\
.find_all('td')
```

10. How many columns of data do we have? Print the length of **row_data** by running **print(len(row_data))**.

11. Print the first elements by running **print(row_data[:4])**:

    ```
    >> [<td>2</td>,
    <td style="font-weight: bold; font-size:15px; text-align:left"><a href="/
    world-population/india- population/">India</a></td>,
    <td style="font-weight: bold;">1,339,180,127</td>,
    <td>1.13 %</td>]
    ```

    It's pretty obvious that we want to select list indices 1, 2, and 3. The first data value can be ignored, as it's simply the index.

12. Select the data elements we're interested in parsing by running the following code:

    ```
    d1, d2, d3 = row_data[1:4]
    ```

13. Looking at the **row_data** output, we can find out how to correctly parse the data. We'll want to select the content of the **<a>** element in the first data element, and then simply get the text from the others. Test these assumptions by running the following code:

    ```
    print(d1.find('a').text) print(d2.text) print(d3.text)
    >> India
    >> 1,339,180,127
    >> 1.13 %
    ```

    Excellent! This looks to be working well. Now, we're ready to scrape the entire table.

14. Scrape and parse the table data by running the following code:

    ```
    data = []
    for i, row in enumerate(soup.find_all('tr')): try:
    d1, d2, d3 = row.find_all('td')[1:4] d1 = d1.find('a').text
    d2 = d2.text d3 = d3.text
    data.append([d1, d2, d3]) except:
    print('Error parsing row {}'.format(i))
    >> Error parsing row 0
    ```

    This is quite similar to before, where we try to parse the text and skip the row if there's some error.

15. Print the head of the scraped data by running **print(data[:10])**:

    ```
    >> [['China', '1,409,517,397', '0.43 %'],
    ['India', '1,339,180,127', '1.13 %'],
    ['U.S.', '324,459,463', '0.71 %'],
    ['Indonesia', '263,991,379', '1.10 %'],
    ['Brazil', '209,288,278', '0.79 %'],
    ```

```
['Pakistan', '197,015,955', '1.97 %'],
['Nigeria', '190,886,311', '2.63 %'],
['Bangladesh', '164,669,751', '1.05 %'],
['Russia', '143,989,754', '0.02 %'],
['Mexico', '129,163,276', '1.27 %']]
```

It looks like we have managed to scrape the data! Notice how similar the process was for this table compared to the Wikipedia one, even though this web page is completely different. Of course, it will not always be the case that data is contained within a table, but regardless, we can usually use **find_all** as the primary method for parsing.

16. Finally, save the data to a CSV file for later use. Do this by running the following code:

```
f_path = '../data/countries/populations.csv' with open(f_path, 'w') as f:
f.write('{};{};{}\n'.format(*table_headers)) for d in data:
f.write('{};{};{}\n'.format(*d))
```

Activity 4: Exploring Data with Interactive Visualizations

1. In the **lesson-3-workbook.ipynb** file, scroll to the **Activity B: Interactive visualizations with Bokeh** section.

2. Load the previously scraped, merged, and cleaned web page data by running the following code:

```
df = pd.read_csv('../data/countries/merged.csv')
df['Date of last change'] = pd.to_datetime(df['Date of last change'])
```

3. Recall what the data looks like by displaying the DataFrame:

	Country	Population	Yearly Change	Interest rate	Date of last change
0	China	1.409517e+09	0.43	1.75	2015-10-23
1	India	1.339180e+09	1.13	6.00	2017-08-02
2	United States	3.244595e+08	0.71	1.25	2017-06-14
3	Indonesia	2.639914e+08	1.10	4.75	2016-10-20
4	Brazil	2.092883e+08	0.79	7.25	2017-07-26
...	...	...	...	...	...
76	Mauritius	1.265138e+06	0.24	4.00	2016-07-20
77	Fiji	9.055020e+05	0.75	0.50	2011-11-02
78	Bahamas	3.953610e+05	1.06	4.00	2016-12-22
79	Iceland	3.350250e+05	0.77	4.50	2017-06-14
80	Samoa	1.964400e+05	0.67	0.14	2016-07-01

81 rows × 5 columns

Figure 3.18: Output of the data within DataFrame

Whereas in the previous exercise we were interested in learning how Bokeh worked, now we are interested in what this data looks like. In order to explore this dataset, we are going to use interactive visualizations.

4. Draw a scatter plot of the population as a function of the interest rate by running the following code:

```
source = ColumnDataSource(data=dict( x=df['Interest rate'],
y=df['Population'], desc=df['Country'],
))
hover = HoverTool(tooltips=[ ('Country', '@desc'),
('Interest Rate (%)', '@x'), ('Population', '@y')
])
tools = [hover, PanTool(), BoxZoomTool(), WheelZoomTool(), ResetTool()]
p = figure(tools=tools,
x_axis_label='Interest Rate (%)', y_axis_label='Population')
p.circle('x', 'y', size=10, alpha=0.5, source=source) show(p)
```

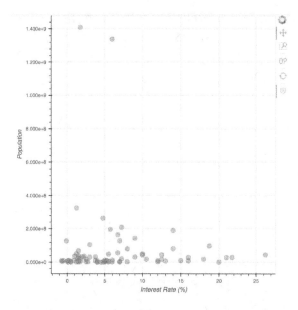

Figure 3.19: Scatter plot of population and interest rate

This is quite similar to the final examples we looked at when introducing Bokeh in the previous exercise. We set up a customized data source with the x and y coordinates for each point, along with the country name. This country name is passed to the Hover Tool, so that it's visible when hovering the mouse over the dot. We pass this tool to the figure, along with a set of other useful tools.

5. In the data, we see some clear outliers with high populations. Hover over these to see what they are:

Figure 3.20: Labels obtained by hovering over data points

We see they belong to India and China. These countries have fairly average interest rates. Let's focus on the rest of the points by using the Box Zoom tool to modify the view window size.

6. Select the Box Zoom tool and alter the viewing window to better see the majority of the data:

Figure 3.21: The Box Zoom tool

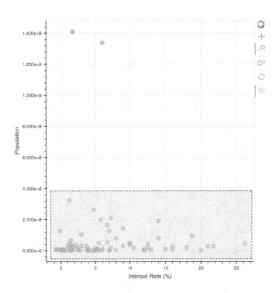

Figure 3.22: Scatter plot with majority of the data points within the box

Explore the points and see how the interest rates compare for various countries. What are the countries with the highest interest rates?:

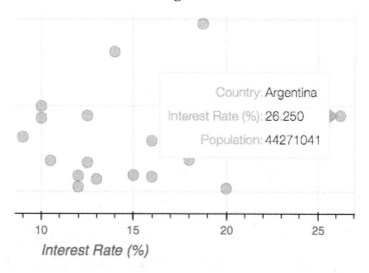

Figure 3.23: Hovering over data points to view detailed data

7. Some of the lower population countries appear to have negative interest rates. Select the **Wheel Zoom** tool and use it to zoom in on this region. Use the **Pan** tool to re-center the plot, if needed, so that the negative interest rate samples are in view. Hover over some of these and see what countries they correspond to:

Figure 3.24: Screen shot of the Wheel Zoom tool

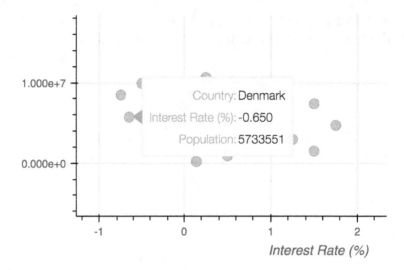

Figure 3.25: Data points of negative interest rates countries

Let's re-plot this, adding a color based on the date of last interest rate change. This will be useful to search for relations between the date of last change and the interest rate or population size.

8. Add a **Year of last change** column to the DataFrame by running the following code:

```
def get_year(x):
year = x.strftime('%Y')
if year in ['2018', '2017', '2016']:
return year else: return 'Other'
df['Year of last change'] = df['Date of last change']. apply(get_year)
```

9. Create a map to group the last change date into color categories by running the following code:

```
year_to_color = { '2018': 'black',
'2017': 'blue',
'2016': 'orange',
'Other':'red'
}
```

Once mapped to the **Year of last change** column, this will assign values to colors based on the available categories: 2018, 2017, 2016, and Other. The colors here are standard strings, but they could alternatively by represented by hexadecimal codes.

10. Create the colored visualization by running the following code:

```
source = ColumnDataSource(data=dict( x=df['Interest rate'],
...
...
fill_color='colors', line_color='black', legend='label')
show(p)
```

> **Note**
>
> For the complete code, refer to the following: https://bit.ly/2Si3K04

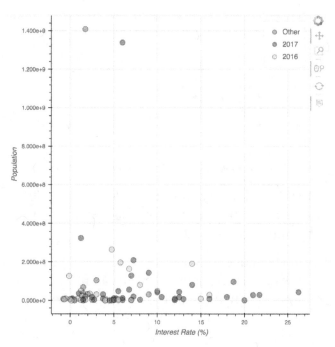

Figure 3.26: Visualization obtained after assigning values to colors

There are some technical details that are important here. First of all, we add the colors and labels for each point to the **ColumnDataSource**. These are then referenced when plotting the circles by setting the **fill_color** and legend arguments.

11. Looking for patterns, zoom in on the lower population countries:

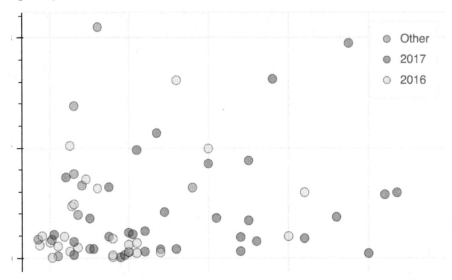

Figure 3.27: A zoomed in view of the lower population countries

We can see how the dark dots are more prevalent to the right-hand side of the plot. This indicates that countries that have higher interest rates are more likely to have been recently updated.

The one data column we have not yet looked at is the year-over-year change in population. Let's visualize this compared to the interest rate and see if there is any trend. We'll also enhance the plot by setting the circle size based on the country population.

12. Plot the interest rate as a function of the year-over-year population change by running the following code:

```
source = ColumnDataSource(data=dict( x=df['Yearly Change'],
...
...
p.circle('x', 'y', size=10, alpha=0.5, source=source, radius='radii')
show(p)
```

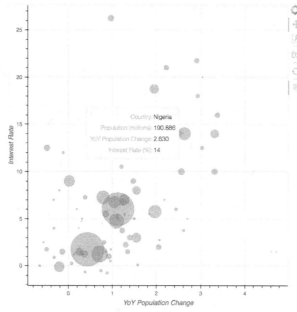

Figure 3.28: Plotting interest rate as a function of YoY population change

Here, we use the square root of the population for the radii, making sure to also scale down the result to a good size for the visualization.

We see a strong correlation between the year-over-year population change and the interest rate. This correlation is especially strong when we take the population sizes into account, by looking primarily at the bigger circles. Let's add a line of best fit to the plot to illustrate this correlation.

We'll use scikit-learn to create the line of best fit, using the country populations (as visualized in the preceding plot) as weights.

13. Determine the line of best fit for the previously plotted relationship by running the following code:

```
from sklearn.linear_model import LinearRegression X = df['Yearly Change'].
values.reshape(-1, 1)
y = df['Interest rate'].values
weights = np.sqrt(df['Population'])/1e5
lm = LinearRegression()
lm.fit(X, y, sample_weight=weights)
lm_x = np.linspace(X.flatten().min(), X.flatten().max(), 50)
lm_y = lm.predict(lm_x.reshape(-1, 1))
```

The scikit-learn code should be familiar from earlier in this book. As promised, we are using the transformed populations, as seen in the previous plot, as the weights. The line of best fit is then calculated by predicting the linear model values for a range of x values.

To plot the line, we can reuse the preceding code, adding an extra call to the **line** module in Bokeh. We'll also have to set a new data source for this line.

14. Re-plot the preceding figure, adding a line of best fit, by running the following code:

```
source = ColumnDataSource(data=dict( x=df['Yearly Change'], y=df['Interest
rate'],
...
...
p.line('x', 'y', line_width=2, line_color='red', source=lm_source)
show(p)
```

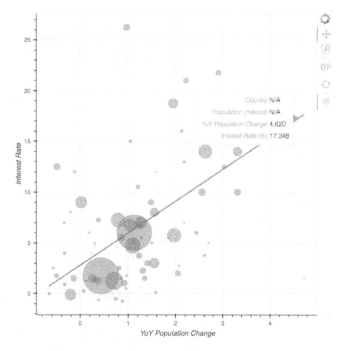

Figure 3.29: Adding a best fit line to the plot of YoY population change and interest rates

For the line source, **lm_source**, we include **N/A** as the country name and population, as these are not applicable values for the line of best fit. As can be seen by hovering over the line, they indeed appear in the tooltip.

The interactive nature of this visualization gives us a unique opportunity to explore outliers in this dataset, for example, the tiny dot in the lower-right corner.

15. Explore the plot by using the zoom tools and hovering over interesting samples. Note the following:

Ukraine has an unusually high interest rate, given the low year-over-year population change:

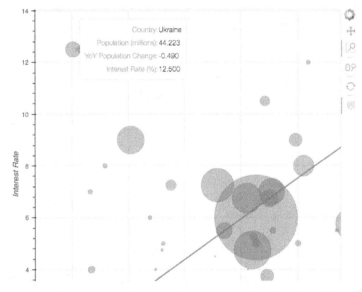

Figure 3.30: Using the Zoom tool to explore the data for Ukraine

The small country of Bahrain has an unusually low interest rate, given the high year-over-year population change:

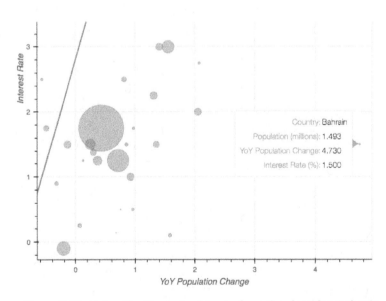

Figure 3.31: Using the Zoom tool to explore the data for Bahrain

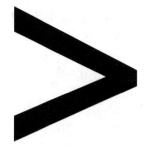

Index

About

All major keywords used in this book are captured alphabetically in this section. Each one is accompanied by the page number of where they appear.

www.ingramcontent.com/pod-product-compliance
Lightning Source LLC
LaVergne TN
LVHW081526050326
832903LV00025B/1641